MONOGRAPHS ON GREENLAND
MEDDELELSER OM GRØNLAND
Vol. 53, no. 5

FACSIMILE
EDITION

William Thalbitzer

The Ammasalik Eskimo

A Rejoinder

MUSEUM TUSCULANUM PRESS
UNIVERSITY OF COPENHAGEN
2010

William Thalbitzer
The Ammasalik Eskimo
A Rejoinder

Facsimile Edition © Museum Tusculanum Press, 2010
Cover design: Erling Lynder
ISBN 978 87 635 2270 0
eISBN 978 87 635 3459 8

Original print edition, Copenhagen, 1917

Monographs on Greenland | Meddelelser om Grønland
Vol. 53, no. 5
ISSN 0025 6676

www.mtp.dk/MoG

Published with financial support from
The Commission for Scientific Research in Greenland.

Museum Tusculanum Press
University of Copenhagen
126 Njalsgade, DK-2300 Copenhagen S
DENMARK
www.mtp.dk

MONOGRAPHS ON GREENLAND | MEDDELELSER OM GRØNLAND

ABOUT THE SERIES

Monographs on Greenland | Meddelelser om Grønland (ISSN 0025 6676) has published scientific results from all fields of research on Greenland since 1878. The series numbers more than 345 volumes comprising more than 1250 titles.

In 1979 Monographs on Greenland | Meddelelser om Grønland was developed into a tripartite series consisting of Bioscience (ISSN 0106-1054), Man & Society (ISSN 0106-1062), and Geoscience (ISSN 0106-1046).

Monographs on Greenland | Meddelelser om Grønland was renumbered in 1979 ending with volume no. 206 and continued with volume no. 1 for each subseries. As of 2008 the original Monographs on Greenland | Meddelelser om Grønland numbering is continued in addition to the subseries numbering.

Further information about the series, including addresses of the scientific editors of the subseries, can be found at www.mtp.dk/MoG.

MANUSCRIPTS SHOULD BE SENT TO

Museum Tusculanum Press
University of Copenhagen
126 Njalsgade, DK-2300 Copenhagen S
DENMARK
info@mtp.dk | www.mtp.dk
Tel. +45 353 29109 | Fax +45 353 29113
VAT no.: 8876 8418

ORDERS

Books can be purchased online at www.mtp.dk, via order@mtp.dk, through any of our distributors in the US, UK, and France or via online retailers and major booksellers. Museum Tusculanum Press bank details: Amagerbanken, DK-2300 Copenhagen S, BIC: AM BK DK KK, IBAN: DK10 5202 0001 5151 08.

DISTRIBUTORS

USA & Canada: ISBS International Specialized Book Services, 920 NE 58th Ave. Suite 300 - Portland, OR 97213, Phone: +1 800 944 6190 (toll-free), Fax: +1 503 280 8832, orders@isbs.com

United Kingdom: Gazelle Book Services Ltd., White Cross Mills, High Town, GB-Lancaster LA1 4XS, United Kingdom, Phone: +44 1524 68765, Fax: +44 1524 63232, sales@gazellebooks.co.uk

France: Editions Picard, 82, rue Bonaparte, F-75006 Paris, France, Phone: +33 (0) 1 4326 9778, Fax: +33 1 43 26 42 64, livres@librairie-picard.fr

V.

THE AMMASSALIK ESKIMO

A REJOINDER

BY

WILLIAM THALBITZER

I. The Explanation.

> In the practice of mutual aid, which we can retrace to the earliest beginnings of evolution, we thus find the positive and undoubted origin of our ethical conceptions; and we can affirm that *in the ethical progress of man, mutual support — not mutual struggle — has had the leading part.*
>
> P. KROPOTKIN, Mutual Aid a factor of evolution.

In 1914, the first part of my work on the heathen East Greenlanders appeared under the general title of "The Ammassalik Eskimo" and with sub-title: "Contributions to the Ethnology of the East Greenland Natives"[1]. The first portion of this volume consisted of an English translation of an earlier work on the Ammassalimmiut, by Kommandør GUSTAV HOLM, the discoverer of the region in question, containing also some papers by various other writers dealing with the same Eskimo tribe. The volume closed with my description of the ethnographical collections from East Greenland affording illustration of the culture of this same people; the collections themselves are preserved in the Ethnographical Department of the National Museum at Copenhagen. My description of these, which was mainly intended as a broader exposition of HOLM's previous commentary on his ethnographical collection, was supplemented by material from my own and other collections and observations from the same part of Greenland.

In an Introduction to this detailed description, I proffered some explanatory remarks concerning my preliminary studies, and the collections which I had consulted. I took the opportunity also, of expressing my thanks to the Museums concerned, in the following words:

"My thanks are due to all the Museums I have visited for the facilities offered me. It is with pleasure that I remember my visits to the ethnographical Museums in Berlin (1904, 1907 and 1912), Vienna (1908), Christiania (1908), Stockholm (1908 and 1910), London (1909) and Dublin (1909). Among these Museums I was obliged naturally to pay special attention to Stockholm's Riksmuseum owing to its excellent collections from Greenland connected with the names of PFAFF (North-West Greenland, inventory completed 1878), N. O

[1] In Meddelelser om Grønland, Vol. XXXIX, Copenhagen 1914.

HOLST (South-West Greenland, 1880), G. v. DÜBEN (West Greenland, 1881) and A. E. NORDENSKJÖLD (East and West Greenland, 1873, 1883, 1885, 1896). I must express my heartiest thanks to the keeper of the Museum, Professor C. V. HARTMAN, for the effective kindness with which, in true comprehension of the difficulty of my research, he facilitated the study of these collections during my repeated visits in Stockholm.

My thanks to the National Museum of Copenhagen cannot rise to the same level of heartiness. The materials contained in this Museum are undoubtedly the most considerable existing, for a study of the ethnography of Greenland. Only a part of them are said to have been set up in cases. I was acquainted with the contents of these cases, but only as a general visitor, when "Commissionen for Grønlands geologiske og geografiske Undersøgelser" in 1907 authorised me to publish a description of the Amdrup collection from East Greenland[1] in its "Meddelelser om Grønland". As a natural and necessary link in carrying out this purpose it seemed desirable to have a new illustration and edition of G. Holm's collection from Ammassalik, which has lain in our National Museum since 1888. I directed a request therefore in 1908 to the director of the ethnographic section, Dr. SOPHUS MÜLLER, that I might be permitted to study the collections from East Greenland, and first and foremost G. HOLM's. In the following year I asked to be allowed to photograph Holm's collection[2]. In the spring of 1910 I succeeded at length in beginning the work of photographing, which extended over 16 days. The work was carried out in front of the cases in the Museum, where the light conditions were not exactly good, by a photographer recommended by the Director and somewhat hastily owing to the short working hours of the Museum. I was present, of course, when all the photographs were taken, but obtained very little time to study the objects taken from the cases, as they had to be brought out and put in again each day by one of the assistants.

When the work was completed, I felt no inducement to continue my studies at this Museum, having the distinct impression, that my visits were unwelcome. I regret, that such a short measure of interest and friendliness obliged me to renounce a fuller utilisation of the rich collections and has thus without doubt reduced the strength of my work. On the other hand, I have had the good fortune of being able to fill up the gap to some extent by my journeys to foreign Museums, which the Carlsberg Fund with great liberality has supported"

These few passages from my book (1914, pp. 328—329) — a single page in a work of some seven hundred and fifty — were intended not only to remind the reader of the extent to which ethnographical material from Greenland is scattered about the world, but also to point out certain difficulties which I had had to encounter on coming in contact with the one particular Museum possessing the greatest store of such material. My remarks concerning the Ethnographical Department at Copenhagen

---

[1] "The Amdrup collection, which has been procured through the Carlsberg Fund Expedition to East Greenland, was at that time still in the possession of the Carlsberg Fund, though promised to the National Museum as soon as its description was ended".

[2] "It may be mentioned in this connection, that in 1897 already there was some talk of getting Holm's collection photographed, arising out of a private request from the well-known ethnographer OTIS MASON of the Washington National Museum, but the director of the Copenhagen Museum neglected to answer".

were designed to intimate the reason why I had curtailed my visits to that Department as far as I honestly could; the fact itself I felt constrained to mention, as accounting for certain failings in my work. My remarks, then, were meant in self-defence, and not aggressively. The effect, however, was surprising; the Museum Department took them as a challenge.

I am not authorised to reveal the manner in which the wrath of the Department was first visited upon myself; the present pages are concerned exclusively with Hr. Underinspektør THOMAS THOMSEN's criticism of my work. The form and tone of the critique in question leave no room for doubt as to its being the direct outcome of this animus; I am therefore called upon to refute, not the unbiassed expression of expert opinion, but the charges of a conscious adversary.

There are not lacking in Hr. THOMSEN's paper utterances indicative of the fact that he is acting at the instigation of departmental authority[1]. Even so, I fail to see on what grounds I should bow to his commission, since I consider him incompetent to deliver judgement on the crucial point of the case.

This crucial point is, of course, my personal relations with our Ethnographical Department, or, more correctly, the attitude of the Department towards myself as visitor and student. The treatment meted out to me by the Department was of such a nature as to prejudice my work, not least through the impressions which I carried away after my studies in this section of the Museum.

Hr. THOMSEN is, I maintain, incompetent to judge at all in this matter, as he was never present at such times as I was occupied in his section, and cannot therefore testify to the manner in which I was received and treated there. At the time when most of my visits took place, the Specialist of the Ethnographical Department happened to be busied about the duties of his office in other parts of the building. I have thus had no intercourse with this gentleman; I do not know him. And I have accordingly no intention of discussing the personal side of the case with Hr. THOMSEN.

I reiterate, however, that my work has been seriously delayed and impaired through the unfriendly reception accorded me by the Ethnographical Department. None of the errors or failings in my book — not even such as might appear to lie beyond the sphere of museum investigation — but was in some measure due to the undermining effects of this hostility.

And I further maintain, that I could not in fairness have formulated any other expression of thanks to the Director of the Museum Department, regrettable as this may seem. In giving my name to the book as its author, I was obviously obliged to explain, what I had realised before its completion, that it contained certain shortcomings, and

[1] e. g. in his paper pp. *382* (bottom of page), *422* and *425* (middle).

I intimated, on the last page of the work, that I understood wherein they chiefly lay. My consciousness of this, however, did not cause me very great anxiety, as I presumed that the errors would prove to be comparatively insignificant from the ethnographical point of view, nor have I since found any reason to think otherwise.

Hr. THOMSEN insists, for his part, that the Museum authorities cannot disregard these failings, the majority of which might easily have been avoided if I had gone to the Museum with a "list of the numbers" i. e. the inventory numbers with which the various objects are marked (p. *387*, cf p. *385*). What is here implied, of course, is that I had neglected to avail myself of the inventory lists.

In all the museums which I visited abroad, the inventory lists were courteously placed at my disposal; in some cases even before I had asked to see them. On seeking the assistance of our own Museum at home, however, I found that this source of knowledge, as regards the Ethnographical Department, constituted a sort of esoteric artesian well, closed down and sealed with seven seals, its contents only to be elicited in drops, and upon written application to the Director's Office. For reasons intimately connected with the crucial point before mentioned, I did not wish to pursue my studies further at the Museum after the work of photographing the East Greenland specimens was completed. The acquisition of these photographs I considered indispensable, as the minimum upon which I could undertake the task of preparing a book on the East Greenland Collections, and I regret that I was forced to be content with such a minimum.

Now omitting certain portions of Hr. THOMSEN's paper, which consists for the most part of longwinded fantasias upon themes from mine, we find that the remainder actually does give a quantity of good and concise information, drawn directly from these very lists. His paper shows, in several instances, that such ethnographical ledgers really may be useful to the student, not least on account of the valuable information they frequently contain as to the origin and purpose of specimens.

Hr. THOMSEN's paper thus indirectly serves to show how much I have lost by venturing within the precincts of our Ethnographical Museum, where I felt myself, only too soon, constrained to desist from further study.

As, however, the effects undoubtedly extended far beyond the mere weakening of my museum work, the scientific loss involved cannot be gauged by Hr. THOMSEN's indications. I am at any rate unable to accept his judgement concerning the shortcomings, real or conjectural, of my book, as an adequate estimate of the detriment suffered. In expressing my regret that the attitude of the Museum had thus "without doubt reduced the strength of my work" (my book 1914 p. 329) I was, it is true, also referring to such failings as have since been pointed out in Hr. THOMSEN's paper (he has thus, in a way, on behalf of his Department, explained the nature and extent of the loss). But my remarks concerned also, indirectly, losses which are for myself personally of a far more serious character.

It is a question — to which I shall revert later on — whether Hr. THOMSEN's criticisms are of any scientific importance. I cannot but repeat here, that the manner in which my critic, in his "Notes and Corrections", deals with the work thus annotated and corrected, is biased and aggressive; any possible merits of the work reviewed are thus entirely ignored. It is a part of his tactical method to exaggerate the scientific importance of such mishaps as arose from my experiences in the Museum, as for instance where an article has been incorrectly assigned to this or that collection. The main point, it need hardly be said, is that objects shown or mentioned should actually be from the region concerned, and truly indicative of the native culture there prevailing. And that my work has achieved its aim in this respect is, I venture to opine, beyond all doubt.

My illustrations, and the text thereto pertaining, contain nothing but true examples of "Ammassalik culture". If certain positive data from the inventories are lacking — and Hr. THOMSEN appears to show a considerable number — these are nevertheless of such a nature that while they might have supplemented my description of the objects in regard to certain minor points, their absence is of slight import in viewing the culture of Ammassalik as a whole. — My critic had here, as an official of the Museum, very obvious advantages as against myself, and has enjoyed the privileges of his office for many years. For this reason also, he must necessarily be incompetent to judge of the case, having never himself been able to view the Department as a visitor, dependent upon the will and pleasure of the Director or his subordinates, nor even himself been present during my visits there.

We see him, then, seated at the very fount of knowledge, criticising and correcting; proffering, with a certain hauteur, the information which I endeavoured to obtain seven years ago.

Hr. THOMSEN's opus thus serves — strangely enough, since I do not know him personally — to confirm still further in its own way my earlier impression of Museum manners in this Department. I recognise, in the satiric style of his work, an echo from the days of my visits to his Department. The tone is in essentials the same, resonant of the very spirit with which I was received within those precincts — and which drove me thence. Evidently, the administrative influence of the Department is highly calculated to permeate and mould the personality of those who are for any length of time subjected to its sway.

II. Promises and Results.

My work has thus given rise to the publication — by the Ethnographical Department of the Museum — of a paper, 55 pages long, concerning the Greenland collections and other matters first dealt with by me. Truly a sudden ebullition of interest in the ethnography of Greenland! This is in fact the first time that one of the Department's officials has issued a work containing scientific details concerning the Greenland material and utilising the inventory lists. Save for the scientifically insignificant "catalogues" which are sold for sixpence at the door, nothing has hitherto been made public by the Department with regard to the large collections from Greenland preserved in the Museum, and chiefly of ancient date. The earliest departmental effort in this direction is now seen in Hr. THOMSEN's critical essay on my ethnographical works, whereby his privileged position, with immediate access to the sources, at last proves of some use to the cause of science.

The publication of my book has evidently fired the blood of our museum-ethnographers, and Hr. THOMSEN rises as their spokesman.

It will be somewhat of a mystery to most, why Hr. THOMSEN in the heading of his paper should wish to alter the title which I had given my book; to wit, "The Ammassalik Eskimo", not, as in his orthography, "Angmagsalik". My spelling is based upon long years of experience in the Greenland tongue, and I had good reasons for preferring the form chosen to that which happens to be authorised. Hr. THOMSEN's heading "The Angmagsalik Eskimo" gives a misleading alteration of my title, not to mention its seeming to claim for his little appendix the position of a counterpart to the work issued by myself concerning the tribe in question.

As to how far Hr. THOMSEN's "Notes and Corrections" furnish any grounds for supposing that he could have carried out the task which fell to my lot with better result than I have attained under the conditions prevailing and during the time available, this I leave others to decide.

Hr. THOMSEN must be content to admit that my work is in reality the first broad survey of Greenland ethnography in existence. He himself apparently does not know what it is to have published an ethnographical work, or indeed a considerable work on any subject, and he does not appear to realise how much more difficult is the work of a pioneer than that of a critic scrutinising along his track.

It may, however, not be out of place to call to mind how it was that I came to undertake a work of this specially ethnographical character.

On my return from a winter in Greenland (1906) I was invited by the Committee for Geological and Geographical Investigations in Greenland, and by the Director of the Carlsberg Fund, to undertake the description of the collections from East Greenland recently brought home to Copenhagen, and of which nothing had been published up to that date. I was the first man in this country since the days of G. Holm, who had taken sufficient scientific interest in the culture of Greenland to learn the language and take up residence among the natives. Nevertheless, I hesitated to accept the honour of such a task. I had at that time published nothing beyond a book on the phonetics of the Eskimo tongue, in Meddelelser om Grønland (Vol. 31, 1904) which had called forth several reviews, all of an appreciative character, in specialist publications. I was now afforded a prospect of extending my sphere of work to a field in which no great scientific work on Greenland had appeared. Dr. H. P. Steensby had, however, shortly before published his thesis on the origin of Eskimo culture[1], and I therefore suggested that the proposed work would be likely to interest him. The Committee nevertheless maintained that I myself, as the only man who had spent two years among the Eskimo and had learned their language, ought to undertake the work, while the Chairman of the Carlsberg Fund likewise urged it as a natural task for me to undertake.

I myself did not fail to point out that this would necessarily delay the execution of the earlier task entrusted to me by these same institutions, to wit, the publication of my linguistic and folkloristic material from Ammassalik, in which, moreover, I was more keenly interested, having myself procured the matter from the traditions of the Ammassalimmiut. I recognised, however, that it might be useful for the linguist to take up a branch of ethnography as an auxiliary; the two tasks might well be prosecuted side by side to mutual advantage. I was well aware that a considerable amount of previous study would be required, in respect of which I should have to seek recourse to the ethnographical side. But it never occurred to me to doubt that in the arena of science, the principle of mutual support must rise superior to that of every man for himself. I had up to that time no grounds for thinking otherwise. It is this I refer to in the introduction to my work of 1909 (p. 334):

"I hesitated at first to undertake work of a kind which lay outside the special line of study I had hitherto pursued. On the other hand, I was moved by the consideration that the publication of the Amdrup collection had already been sufficiently delayed. This interesting collection surely deserved a better fate than to be forgotten. Further than this, in my capacity of linguist, I was sensible of the advantage of obtaining a better insight into the forms assumed by the material culture of the East Greenlanders; for changes in the implements

[1] Steensby's work has since appeared in an enlarged and translated (English) Edition in vol. 53 of Medd. om Grønland, with the title "An Anthropogeographical study of the Origin of the Eskimo Culture".

often run parallel to changes in the language and the Ammassalimmiut, in fact, have their own particular designations for many of their Eskimo implements and utensils (etc)«.

Finally, then, I agreed to undertake the work, and formulated a proposal for a somewhat extended scheme, to include an English translation of G. HOLM's ethnological work on the East Greenlanders, together with a new description of the most important types of implements in his collection. These additions I regarded as a natural link in the whole. I commenced my studies with confidence and pleasure. I did not then anticipate that my visit to the Ethnographical Department of our Museum was to be productive of most bitter disappointment; so much so indeed, as to cause me after a brief while to withdraw, in voluntary ostracism, from the place.

It is no secret, that Hr. THOMSEN some years back was commissioned to publish a description of the material brought home in 1908 by the Danmark Expedition (the famous voyage of MYLIUS-ERICHSEN and his comrades to the unknown regions of North-east Greenland). It has hitherto been less generally known, however, that the task in question was first offered to *me*, viz: at the same time as the Committee empowered me to deal with the finds of the AMDRUP Expedition from the central and northern part of East Greenland. As it happened, however, the ethnographical collection from the Danmark Expedition had in the meantime been handed over to our National Museum (1st Department), and from that moment, if not before, objections must have been raised by the Ethnographical Department against allowing the new and valuable acquisition to be dealt with by anyone outside the circle of the Museum's ethnographers. On learning that the ethnographers of the Museum were wishful themselves to undertake the description and publication of this collection from the extreme North-east of Greenland, I at once relinquished all claim to the honour, whereby I hoped to have removed all possible grounds for friction, and even, it might be, to have made a step towards securing the good will of the Museum[1].

It was with reference to this situation, that I wrote, in the Introduction to my Description of the Amdrup Collection from N. E. Greenland 1909 (p. 343), as follows:

"These 'finds' have recently been added to. From more northerly districts of East Greenland than ever before, MYLIUS-ERICHSEN and his companions on the Danmark Expedition brought back a collection of antiquities. I have not yet had an opportunity of seeing this collection which immediately after

[1] Naturally, I should never for a moment have thought of intruding upon a scientific domain to which another could with any show of reason advance a prior claim; I had not the least desire to interfere with the handling of ethnographical material already entrusted to other hands.

its arrival was lodged in the National Museum at Copenhagen. It is to be hoped that it will not be long before we get a description of it by a competent hand".

This promised description is still to be looked forward to, and with the same hopes as before. When Hr. THOMSEN's ethnographical work finally does appear, I venture to hope it may be borne in mind, how thoroughly the author has studied mine.

III. "Notes and Corrections" *versus* Scientific Research-work.

With regard to Hr. THOMSEN's "Notes and Corrections", I should be able to regard these with more respect if they were not so markedly redolent of the aggressive tendency before mentioned, which does not even draw the line at personal insinuation. The form of his attack is such that I have the strongest disinclination to answer it at all. I could expose myself wihout a tremor to the shafts of honest criticism loosed by a competent hand. But since becoming acquainted with the contents of his present paper, I can no longer trust his weapons as clean nor his competence as genuine.

My departmental critic has been pleased to dilate upon what he terms "Mr. THALBITZER's peculiar methods of dealing with Museum material" (p. *417*)[1]. I have no idea as to what may be Hr. THOMSEN's method of dealing with Museum material. But I cannot accept his estimate of the various East Greenland collections in the Museum; his presentment of these appears to me misleading from the very commencement of his paper.

A false impression is created at the outset by the manner in which RYDER's collection from Ammassalik is referred to as if it were one well known to the public. Hr. THOMSEN endeavours to make this apparent by a footnote (No. 2) on p. *381*, citing Medd. om Grønland vol. 17 p. 138 ff; there is, however, here no mention whatever of the fact that RYDER ever made any collection at all, still less that any such was contributed by him to the Museum. Even more remarkable is the fact that the Museum catalogue does not contain — or did not at the time of my visits there — any reference to the presence in the Museum of a collection from Ammassalik made by RYDER. No notices to such effect were hung up in the rooms, nor was there so much as a card in

[1] In the following pages, when citing Hr. THOMSEN's paper, the page numbers in this will be set in italics; references to my own work, Meddel. om Grønl. vol. 39, 1914 in black type.

the cases calling attention thereto[1]. For the purpose of my work, I had made every endeavour to obtain information as to all collections which might serve to illustrate the culture of Ammassalik, and obviously no one could be more interested than myself in knowing that there was a collection of RYDER's from Ammassalik, and this, moreover, exhibited in the large East Greenland case in our National Museum. I was unable, however, to ascertain this fact, which appears to have been known only to the collector and the official ethnographer of the Department. I naturally supposed all the exhibits in this case, and particularly all such objects as occupied a prominent position there, to have originated from HOLM's expedition to Ammassalik, except where otherwise indicated by special cards. I did not doubt, for instance, that this was the case with the complete sets of men's and women's clothing in the centre, as shown in my Figs. 294 to 300 and 304 to 310. Hr. THOMSEN now informs me that I was here labouring under a delusion. True, I was right in taking the dresses as belonging to the culture of Ammassalik, and it is likewise correct that HOLM collected a great number of them, but part of the material was, Hr. THOMSEN informs us, subsequently contributed by RYDER and JOHAN PETERSEN. The same, I understand, also applies to a number of other articles anonymously exhibited in the large East Greenland case at the Museum, and shown in my illustrations. My note: "Holm coll." under the figures is thus in certain cases incorrect, owing to my not having been able to procure this information earlier.

It is likewise misleading when Hr. THOMSEN asserts, that "these three collections" — i. e. HOLM's, RYDER's and AMDRUP's — "together serve to illustrate the culture of Angmagsalik at about the time of its discovery" (p. *382*) — The statement is altogether correct only as regards Holm's and Amdrup's collections (the last-named from Nualik) both of which date from the time immediately before or immediately after the discovery of the Ammassalimmiut, whereas Ryder's collection was hastily made eight years after Holm's wintering there.

By this I do not in the least mean to assert that RYDER's collection from Ammassalik is valueless; it is even probable that there may, among the duplicates in this collection of the HOLM collection, be found some new forms and variations characteristic of the East Greenlanders. It is unwarrantable, however, to rank this collection, got together in the space of a fortnight, and made up largely of duplicates and articles

[1] Only such portions of RYDER's collections as were brought from Scoresby Sound were indicated by special cards in the museum cases, and have been made known to the public by RYDER's own frequently cited work on the earlier Eskimo occupants at Scoresby Sound, in Medd. om Grønl. vol. 17 (1895) pp. 281—343. In my ethnographical description of the northern finds in the AMDRUP Collection (ed. 1909) I have given all due credit to this work of RYDER's, and have also repeatedly referred to the same in my last work.

made to order, with the older collection, which was made in the very year of the discovery during the course of a winter's stay, or with one like AMDRUP's, consisting of antiquities from a deserted region of the coast.

RYDER himself moreover, takes quite another view of his collection from Ammassalik than of his material from the northern part of the coast (Scoresby Sound). The latter he has subjected to an excellent and exhaustive special investigation, whereas he makes only casual mention of the former in the report of his expedition along the East Coast, wintering at Scoresby Sound and touching for a short stay at Ammassalik. There is no statement in his report as to his having brought new forms of implements or other unknown objects from Ammassalik[1]. There is a brief and incidental mention[2] of the fact that certain pieces of needlework were ordered, and that an indefinite number of ethnographical specimens were obtained by barter on board the ship, these including the clothing ordered, etc. but no suggestion that this should serve to supplement, for instance, the Holm collection.

From the ethnographical point of view, the names of collectors can hardly be regarded as of primary importance. My selection from the various collections is such, that I can confidently recommend the illustrations in my book to anyone wishing to obtain a true idea as to the material culture of the Ammassalik Eskimo at the close of the period when this place was still in a state of isolation, or nearly so. Thus the term "Holm Collection" in my work must be taken as collectively indicating the oldest collections from Ammassalik; in some instances moreover (comprising in all 16 objects) including also articles of earlier origin in the Museum than the contributions from HOLM's expedition, and derived from the nearest stretch of coast south of Ammassalik[3]; in others, indicating duplicates subsequently received.

Hr. THOMSEN thus assigns to the RYDER collection a somewhat

---

[1] With regard to this place, RYDER had instructions to investigate, as far as possible, certain principle questions regarding the natives; e. g. whether they were acquainted with the use of the axe, as known elsewhere among the Eskimo. None such were found by HOLM at Ammassalik, nor any by Ryder (l. c. 138).

[2] RYDER l. c. pp. 130 and 135—36.

[3] These are, according to Hr. THOMSEN's inventories, illustrated in the following figures in my book: Fig. 187 b Shark's tooth knife (GRAAH 1829); 192 b Finger-protector (RYBERG 1883); 273 Water bottle of wood (KIELSEN 1849); 280 c Water tub (KIELSEN 1849); 293 c and d Women's inner breeches (*c* HØYER 1865, d HOLBØLL 1846); 309 Women's dress (the frock, KIELSEN 1849, the breeches, RINK 1854, the boots, HOLBØLL 1850); 316 Eye-shades with ivory relief work (*d* KIELSEN 1840, g HOLBØLL 1844, h JESSEN 1881, i HOLBØLL 1838); 325 c Woman's necklace, fragment (HOLM 1881); 392 Week Calender made of wood (1848); 393 Seal rattles (*a* or *b*? HØYER 1865). — In fig. 350 b is shown a wooden object (amulet board?) from Ungudlik in Julianehaab district, nearly akin to East Greenlandic culture.

over-prominent place; strangely enough, however, he omits from his description (p. *382*) JOHAN PETERSEN's large and valuable private collection, acquired by the State for the Museum — at the request of the Director — in the year 1910, when the collector was in Copenhagen on leave, after 18 years' residence in his official capacity at Ammassalik. This collection is nevertheless probably superior in several respects to RYDER's, having been made after careful preparation, with the chance of fortunate finds, and by one excellently acquainted with the natives of the place. JOHAN PETERSEN's name is mentioned, it is true, but his collection deserved special note in this connection, quite as well as RÜTTEL's and ROSING's collections of a single speciality (amulets)[1].

Plan and Contents of the Work.

p. *383*. — Hr. THOMSEN here asserts, in his somewhat lofty style, that "The task entrusted to the Editor . . . was briefly and plainly this . . ." etc. He also refers to "the confusion which is thus apparent in the plan of the work". Now what does Hr. THOMSEN know of the task which was entrusted to me after my return from my investigations in East Greenland? It should already be evident to him, from the foregoing, that he had but an incomplete and partly incorrect idea of the same. And if I were to make public the plan of the whole work, including the translated edition of HOLM's book, which I laid before the Committee, at the request of the Chairman, on the occasion of the Committee Meeting in April 1907, and which, after having been accepted and recommended to the consideration of the Carlsberg Fund, was further supported by the same until the publication of my work in 1914 — he would be forced to take another view of "the task entrusted" to me from the very commencement[2]. All that he states with regard to this (p. *383—384*) shows, that *he* considers the task too great, and that he at the same time does not know what he is talking about.

The matter dealt with in my work is, as the mere table of contents will suffice to show, arranged on clear and distinct lines. The confusion which my critic finds therein must be due to the quality of his own intelligence. I followed a principle similar to that observed by G. HOLM in his original edition; viz: that of placing the ethnographical

---

[1] JOHAN PETERSEN's collection is casually mentioned in a footnote later on (p. *394*).

[2] My work contains, in the first place, what it was intended to contain according to the plan laid down. As regards the anthropology, I may refer to the section: Contributions to the Anthropology of the East Greenlanders, by SØREN HANSEN, in my book (1914) pp. 149–179. In the second place, the work contains in certain respects more material than the original scheme could possibly have anticipated. How can the work have deteriorated from the fact that the material in course of treatment grew richer and more up to date?

illustrations in a special section of the work, at the end (in the original edition on plates). I consider my description of the ethnography of the Ammassalik Eskimo (Section VII) as an extension of the brief notes appended by HOLM to his plates. Here, where I had a mass of illustrative material drawn from several different collections, I preferred to distribute the figures throughout the text, grouping them, of course, according to a natural classification.

When Hr. THOMSEN observes (p. *384*) that "HOLM's treatise appears no longer as an independent work, but as an appendix" he is following a very devious train of thought; HOLM's pioneer work could never be regarded by any sensible scientist as an appendix, either to my book or to any other. If either of the two should be designated as an appendix, it must be mine; even here, however, the term would be incorrect, since my description forms a natural continuation of HOLM's, and is an independent contribution. In this the treatment of HOLM's ethnographical material has been supplemented by other matter from the same locality or from the neighbouring coast region to the south; I made a selection to the best of my judgment from the private collections or museums to which I had access. Had I omitted these collections, (other than HOLM's and AMDRUP's) my description would have been incomplete.

Thanks to my selection of the ethnographical material, the new edition of HOLM's famous book is now accompanied by augmented and more modern illustrations of the material culture of Ammassalik. It is obviously an advantage, that it also includes some specimens of the culture of the southern East Coast, which is so nearly allied to that of Ammassalik, even though the Museum inventory cannot furnish exact information in each particular case as to the locality on the East Coast whence these 16 specimens are derived. In a description of the culture of South-East Greenland, however, it is of minor importance to know the year and locality of origin of these articles, the more so since all are from the time previous to HOLM's expedition up along the East Coast. Ninety-nine percent of my illustrations are from the higher region of this culture, the fjords of Ammassalik and Sermilik, and the remainder from the neighbouring tract of coast to the south. The Museum critic might have spared himself the carping remarks as to my illustrations having been "drawn from different collections varying considerably in point of time and place". The strength of my work has at any rate suffered nothing from this particular fact.

Treatment of the Museum Material.

p. *385—88*. — The reason why I did not make use of the Museum inventory lists has been shown in the foregoing (p. 440). I can have but little pleasure in expressing my thanks for information received seven years too late.

On p. *385* $_{20\text{-}21}$. — Hr. THOMSEN observes that "The Author 'feels some uncertainty in this respect' regarding ten illustrations in the text". This is a misunderstanding. It would be far more correct to say, that I felt a general uncertainty as to referring the objects to HOLM's collection, and merely mentioned the ten instances as examples (M. o. G. Vol. 39, p. 755), where the appearance of the objects, or of my photographs, gave me particular reason to doubt.

As already mentioned, the manner in which the exhibits were arranged at the Museum afforded the visitor no guidance; the East Greenland collections from this and the more southerly part of the coast were indiscriminately mingled.

I had no doubt at all, however, as to the essential point, viz: that all these objects were truly representative of Ammassalik culture (in the broader sense), and I considered the question of collectors' names as relatively subordinate.

I may add, moreover, — and I should like to emphasise the point — that since Hr. THOMSEN in several cases admits his inability to identify the specimens shown by me from his Museum (cf. p. 479) it will be reasonable to regard with some mistrust the whole of this side of his work. I have myself handled all these objects; Hr. THOMSEN has only the illustrations in my book to go upon. I may at least decline to be held responsible for his failure to identify certain exhibits, and his inability to do so is no concern of mine.

p. *387*, note *2*. Here, by way of variety, I find myself accused of having followed my authority too closely, i. e. literally. My quotation and reproduction of an illustration from NELSON's work on the Eskimo of Alaska will be found in a little Danish volume dealing with Greenland sagas on the past history of the Eskimo, included in a series of popular, or popularly scientific, ethnographical works published by C. V. HARTMAN (Stockholm). It is in the first place unfortunate, that Hr. THOMSEN should declare the notes under the two plates in NELSON's work to have been transposed, since the notes, as a matter of fact, are where they should be; it is the blocks for the plates which have been changed about (Pl. LIII to face p. 135 and Pl. LVIII to p. 151). Moreover, my illustration is not taken directly from Nelson's work, but is reproduced after a somewhat indistinct copy in another[1]. The details in my figure are therefore somewhat vague, so that it is difficult to discern the exact appearance of the head of the weapon, or to determine whether there is any connection between the lifted weapon and the thin line on the kayak. The only thing that is quite distinct is the slender shape of the throwing stick and its position at the rear end of the spear, which circumstance naturally leads one to suppose that it is a bird spear, in accordance with NELSON's note beneath the figure (though on the other hand, this does not exclude the possibility of its being a sealing harpoon). The fact that the well-known three lateral points are lacking

[1] I have since examined NELSON's original illustration, in order to see whether the details in the kayak and the man's weapons are here more distinct than in the copy. This is naturally also the case; even here, however, the illustration shows evident traces of having been made not from a photograph, but from a drawing.

does not necessarily indicate that the weapon is not a bird spear, vide, e. g. NELSON's own illustration of bird spears (Plate LIX).

In other words, the illustration is not one from which the nature of the weapon can be determined with certainty, even by one well acquainted with Eskimo weapons.

p. *388.* Here we touch upon my illustrations of the 16 specimens from the South-East Coast brought home prior to HOLM's arrival at Ammassalik. Hr. THOMSEN appears to have a particular affection for these articles, albeit their locality of origin in most cases cannot be more nearly decided than as from the neighbouring district south of Ammassalik, between Sermilik and Cape Farewell. Not having access to the Museum inventory lists, I was naturally unable to say more with regard to these objects than what could be learned from examination of the objects themselves. They belong in all essentials to the culture of Ammassalik, and may thus serve to illustrate the same.

Hr. THOMSEN's remarks anent my "fault" is in any case entirely beyond the mark, owing to the distinct bias which it reveals. His favorite statement as to these objects, that they "do not originate from Angmagsalik at all, but from the West Coast" (p. *388*[5]) is altogether futile, since these objects, like many more of East Greenland origin, have been brought to the West Coast by travellers from the eastern side. There is, indeed, nothing at all to preclude the supposition that part of them actually originated from Ammassalik itself, or the neighbouring fjords, as we know to have been the case with other old finds brought to Europe by the same route. Even HOLM's Ammassalik collection reached us via the West Coast.

The Authorities Quoted.

p. *389—393.* — What writer has, prior to myself, endeavoured to contribute to the study of Eskimo culture, from these early literary sources? If any there be, his name is assuredly not THOMSEN.

After eight years spent in studying the ethnography of Greenland, and having all but completed my main work on the subject, I had to consider the question as to what conclusion should be drawn from my comparative investigation. If such a conclusion were to be of any importance, it must necessarily embrace certain historical features; the colonisation of South Greenland by the Norsemen in the Middle Ages, the immigration of the Eskimo and their coming in contact with the Norsemen the early appearance of the Eskimo on both sides of Davis Straits, etc. When nearing the conclusion of my work, my attention was called to a few old literary sources beyond those which I had previously consulted at our public libraries[1]. Had I neglected to include such material as was to be found in these works of ancient date. such

[1] Vid. my book 1914 p. 789 note 2.

as PURCHAS, HAKLUYT, FROBISHER, DAVIS, DE POINCY, Les Relations des Jesuites, CHARLEVOIX, LAHONTAN, etc. etc., I should undoubtedly have rendered myself liable to criticism. Now, when I have not neglected this, Hr. THOMSEN is pleased to criticise me for not having taken enough. He himself appears to have had plenty of time in his museum for a thorough study of my sources here, and the results of his industry make themselves apparent, as usual, in the "correction of errors".

— [Not even printer's errors are beneath his notice; evidently, all is fish that comes to his net. I do not in the least grudge him this pitiful sport; yet I confess I could have wished for a critic better able to distinguish between the trifling and the essential.

Hr. THOMSEN's zeal leads him at times to take advantages of such faults as are patently due to a slip of the pen or even, as indicated, to an oversight in the reading of the proofs. I may here at once point out one or two such instances, since they serve to illustrate his method. The placing of a ("sic") after a printer's error whereby "is" appears instead of the obvious "it" might almost seem to be meant in jest (vid. his paper p. *419*$_{15}$). And surely only wilful misunderstanding could fail to see that the two numbers 561 and 562 in my list of ethnographical collections p. **744**$_{4\text{-}5}$ are a mere typographical slip for 56^1 and 56^2. To class them among "scientific errors", as he does p. *412*$^{7\text{-}8}$, is misleading. The same, with some modification, applies to my *ekalugsaa* from OLEARIUS (cf. p. 467 here), and the date 1789 for 1689 (cf. p. 478). Such errors are always regrettable, but there are few large works in which none such can be found.

Even Hr. THOMSEN's own paper is not free from errors of this sort, more or less important; I will not, however, here waste space on any lengthy list, but content myself with the following observations:

In quoting my work, Hr. THOMSEN now and again introduces, on his own account, printer's errors or mistakes which do not appear there at all, and on the single occasion when he cites the title of my work (the real object of his criticisms!) that title is rendered meaningless by the omission of the last word. I must be permitted here to correct the following erroneous quotations in Hr. THOMSEN's paper:

	Error.	Amendment.
p. *382*$_{\text{note 2}}$	"the East Greenland"	"the East Greenland Natives"
- *413*^{12}	"... a snow beater ..."	"... a snow beater? ..."
- *413*$^{16\text{-}17}$	".... (or toy harpoons?)..	"... (of toy harpoons?) ..."
- *414*^{17}	"Vantissard Island"	"Vansittard Island"
- *420*$_{10}$	"inv. Adm. 17"	"inv. Amd. 17"

On p. *417*, Hr. THOMSEN gives a long passage from my book, tricked out with arbitrary spacing at various points; apparently with the air of extracting some amusement from the text thus deformed

He omits to point out, however, that the peculiar spacing is of his own invention.

On pp. *419—420*, he repeatedly mentions the name of the Swedish ethnographer SWENANDER, with reference to my book. Unfortunately, the name is throughout incorrectly spelt — but this is Hr. THOMSEN's error, and not mine. — On p. *394*[5-6] Hr. THOMSEN states that I have referred fig. 273 incorrectly to HOLM's collection; the reference is however, corrected on p. **755** of my work, and the same applies to several similar cases. — On p. *428* (ad **478**) we find a verb in the singular ("is", etc) used with reference to the contents of my fig. 190, although the reference is to two objects. It is thus doubtful which of the two should be understood. — On p. *429* (ad **512**) he makes mention of a fig. 531c in my book; none such, however, exists, as my figure numbers end with 398].

It was never my intention, I admit, to make an exhaustive investigation into the criticism of sources. What I sought in these old works was ethnographic material, not historical detail, and I still believe that my work is not without some value as having called attention to certain little-known passages bearing on the ethnography of the Eskimo in older times. Even if I have here and there been at fault — which I am the first to regret — my excerpts from the older writers yet contain much correct and noteworthy information of interest from the point of view of historical ethnography.

p. *389*. — My book is intended to deal with the ethnography of the East Greenlanders, and in some degree also to compare the same with that of the West Greenlanders and other Eskimo. (And it should be borne in mind, that no detailed description of the ethnography of the West Greenlanders has yet been written).

My statement as to the number of Greenlanders brought, according to OLEARIUS, to this country from Greenland via Norway, is in accordance with the facts, since I did not include such as died and were buried before reaching here. On p. **436**, I have correctly noted their route as via Bergen; the "via Trondhjem" in Note 2 p. **682** is thus due to a slip of the pen.[1]

On p. *390*[1-2]. —"We are informed by Mr. THALBITZER that he [NICOLAS TUNES] 'landed at 64° 10′ N. lat.'" My critic will not be able to weaken this fact. The figure may be seen in DE POINCY, and appeared to me more essential than the subsequent 72°, since there might from the first be some doubt as to the accuracy of these localities, which were not obtained directly from the Dutch captain, but have only been handed

[1] The same applies to the title of JACOBÆUS' book on the Royal private Museum, which is correctly given, in my "List of works consulted" as *Museum Regium* etc. but which I unfortunately happen to refer to on p. **685** (cf Thomsen p. *392*) as *Theatrum* (instead of Museum) — possibly owing to the fact that the Latin preface to the work commences with the words: "*Theatro* Orbis publico Museum *Regium* se sistit" etc.

down to us through the medium of the author of a work on the West Indies. Less doubt, however, would naturally attach to the figure giving the more detailed indication, the more so when this corresponds to a spot far easier of access by sea than the more northerly one which Hr. THOMSEN prefers. "64° 10′" would correspond exactly to the position of *Godthaab*, the principal landing place in South Greenland, whereas "72°" would be *Upernawik*, the farthest Danish colony to the North, where only comparatively few ships touch. It may be uncertain whether DE POINCY's authority did land at 72° N. lat, but there is some reason to believe that he landed from Godthaab Fjord, and saw the objects described with his own eyes.

p. *390*[19]. — "... that he (Mr. THALBITZER) does not even know on which side of Davis Strait it lies". It is an open question. At the Museum itself they do not know where the Dutch captain (NIC. TUNES) did land.

p. *390—392*. — We have here a typical example of Hr. THOMSEN's somewhat pedantic method of criticism, to wit an eager scraping together of some inessential details, a few accidental inaccuracies, including a printer's error, from my mention of SCHACHT. Possibly I may have done the old compiler too great honour in according him 20 lines of small type; my critic, however, vouchsafes him twice the number. Hr. THOMSEN's observations serve for the most part but to obscure what I had particularly wished to call attention to in this old MS; they suffice, however, to lend him some show of learning for himself. As to the date at which the work was composed, I was, as it happens, not misinformed, as will be seen from the fact that I have correctly stated in the text p. 683, that the writer in question was born in 1660 and died at Kerteminde (Carteminde) in Funen, in 1700, and that my mention of him on the same page commences with the proper date of the MS.[1] Hr. THOMSEN's reference to the "List of writers" found in SCHACHT is as valueless as Schacht's list itself. Altogether misleading is my critic's note p. *391* (no. 1), for LAURIDSEN mentions, in his Greenland Bibliography, not one, but four MSS under the name of SCHACHT, naturally the same which I have noted.[2]

---

[1] My work (1914) p. 683: "In SCHACHT's Manuscript from the end of the 17th century, the illustrations of which are in part identical with those of DE POINCY etc." — The last interesting piece of information anent the illustrations is not denied by my critic.

[2] In P. LAURIDSEN's Bibliographia Groenlandica (Medd. om Grønland vol. 13) we find quoted under Schacht's name four MSS altogether, namely, in Section VIII D p. 156 (1) N. Kgl. S. Fol. no. 1290, p. 157 (2) N. Kgl. S. 4° no. 1965 and p. 158 (3) A. M. 4° no. 775; in Section II (p. 49), the MS (4) A. M. no. 364 Fol. These references are in agreement with the Catalogue of the Old-Icelandic MSS, edited by Kommissionen for det Arnamagnæanske Legat (1909). We have thus a complete original manuscript (from 1689) and three more or less defective copies. It is correct, that

With regard to the Dutchman, PALUDANUS, mentioned in my quotation from OLEARIUS, my critic has found, in a Dutch book, some very interesting information, and I can only advise him to pursue his studies further[1]. He refers, in a footnote, to OLEARIUS' Gottorfische Kunstkammer, without adding that this work was printed in Schleswig 1666. The "Kunstkammer" (private museum) in question was later transferred to Copenhagen, and had I been more cautious, I should not have stated of the remarkable idol from the 17th century, that it was brought to Copenhagen, but only that it came to Denmark (scil. Gottorp). Hr. THOMSEN adds "not from Western Greenland", but OLEARIUS mentions this idol in connection with "der Grünländer Religion" and it would thus be natural to connect the finding of it with DANELL's expeditions, which had then recently brought Denmark into contact with West Greenland (1652—54). — OLEARIUS' well-known "Muskowitische und Persianische Reise", in which the idol is described for the first time (cf. my work p. **683** note 3) was published in 1656, but the illustrations of the idol did not appear until some years later, and not first in SCHACHT's MS (p. 167), where I noticed it, but — and this I had overlooked — in OLEARIUS' second work from 1666, to which Hr. THOMSEN refers me. On comparing these two illustrations I find, that the one in SCHACHT's MS is somewhat larger than that in Olearius, and that it exhibits some slight alterations in the dress (the hair of the furs, the shading, etc.) whence it is evident that Schacht had not cut his figure out of a book. It is drawn with writing ink or indian ink on a slip of paper pasted into the MS, as are the remainder of his illustrations. — I have in my book, likewise on p. **683**, note 3, given the text accompanying the figure from Schacht's MS, in his Latin translation, which now, however, turns out to be a quotation translated from OLEARIUS (1666). Hr. THOMSEN gives the German text, from this book, which answers to the Latin. Naturally, it makes but little difference which we use; SCHACHT's Latin is good enough, and tells us the same as OLEARIUS' German.

p. *393*. I am well aware that the list of earlier writers might be added to, and I have never doubted that a considerable amount of further detail might be drawn from other works than those which happened to be available for my purpose (only, of course, excluding such as repose

A M. 364 is the principal MS, and that it contains less than 200 pp. (there are in all 178, not 192 as Hr. THOMSEN states). The page numbers beyond 100 are, however, all written with an initial figure formed almost like the figure 2, which might easily be misread.

[1] In the footnotes to these pages Hr. THOMSEN exhibits a dainty specimen of his erudition. He appears, by the way, to have overlooked the Danish Historian L. BOBE, who, in his recently published paper "Christian Lunds Relation om Danells tre rejser til Grønland" (Danske Magazin 6. R. 11, 1915, p. 232 note 2) gives this and other information regarding BERNHARD PALUDAN (VAN DEN BROECK), a physician of Enckhuyzen.

in the Library of our Museum Department which I have long since grown to regard as beyond my reach). As it is, however, I never aimed at giving other or more than what I have given in this respect, and I think I may fairly claim that my selection as it stands is extensive enough. Should I, however, have overlooked any source offering valuable ethnographical information, the burden of proof lies with the critic who maintains this is the fact; Hr. Thomsen makes no attempt at proving such to be the case.

Hr. Thomsen is therefore wrong in endeavouring to make it appear that I had in reality aimed at giving a survey of all earlier sources of knowledge as to the lands on either side of Davis Straits ("attempting to give a synopsis of early works" p. *391*[11]) and thereafter slighting the sources given, six in all, as "a very scanty and casual selection". We have here a repetition of the same misleading method in accordance with which he seeks on p. *383*f. (cf. p. 448), to disparage my plan of work by proclaiming his own erroneous idea of what the "task entrusted to the editor" really was, and, by comparing the actual contents with this arbitrary scheme of his own, to prove the existence of "shortcomings" and "confusion".

Hr. Thomsen speaks of my methods ("a certain doubt as to the results which may be arrived at by such methods") as if he considered the correctness of a method a safeguard against slips and printers' errors. It must at least be admitted, that my method has after all led to a certain positive result, whereas Hr. Thomsen's has up to the present produced nothing but a negative criticism of my work. The very contemptuous words in which he speaks of my book appear to indicate a high degree of self-confidence, and hint at a method of quite another sort, of which he is the perfect master, and which is to be made manifest in his own coming work. When this appears, he will have had a certain amount of practice in examining "thoroughly, point by point" the whole of my book; we may thus, it would seem, be justified in expecting that his, in contrast to mine, will not invite such summary condemnation as "loosely written"; "not particularly readable"; and the like.

The History of Ammassalik.

p. *393—394*. — Here the Museum official brings forward a note from his inventory lists, referring to an object procured in South Greenland 1849 and stated as coming from Ammassalik ("Angmarselik"). Thus we are now informed, for the first time, that the name of this place was known to a Dane in Greenland prior to the middle of the last century, about 35 years before any Dane had reached there. This secret has been well preserved at the Museum until now.

In this connection I may add, that the inhabitants of the same part of the East Coast are already mentioned in the literature of the

18th century, by P. C. Walløe and D. Cranz[1], and, as far as I am aware, the next time about 1830 by J. C. Mørch, an official in the Julianehaab district. This last-named writer relates (in "Borgervennen", for 1831, pp. 34—35) that he had himself encountered people from the East Coast (66° N. lat.), but he does not mention the name of their native place. "These people, who had formerly been reckoned as cannibals, were the gentlest creatures [de frommeste Mennesker] one could imagine". We have doubtless here to deal with visitors from the district of Ammassalik. The writer mentions, at the same time, that the East Coast is inhabited as far up as 69° N. lat. (*Kialinek*), his information thus differing from that received by Graah during his voyage along the East Coast in 1830[2].

We have here another confirmation from the earlier literature of the view given by later reports, to the effect that the East Greenlanders, also in some cases the natives of Ammassalik, made journeys to the West Coast several years prior to 1850[3].

A Wooden Bottle from East Greenland.

p. *394—95.* — Owing to the scanty space of time, which — loth as I was to enter the Department at all — I found myself able to devote to study there, I was not in a position thoroughly to examine each separate item or to revise my impression of the Museum collections while compiling my book[4], and it is possible that I may have overlooked one of the three holes in the wooden bottle (only one is seen in my photo). Now, in 1916, the world at large is finally made acquainted with the true state of the case, thanks to the sensational statement of this Museum official.

It should be noted, by the way, that Hr. Thomsen's explanation as to there having originally been a handle with sucking tube passed through the two lateral holes, is drawn from a note (unknown to me) in the Museum inventory, where the native tradition in this case is preserved, but is not to be arrived at from the appearance of the object in question, where the handle is lacking. "Mikeeki's waterscoop" No. 213 in the Petersen collection, which Hr. Thomsen declares to be of the same type, had — if I remember rightly — but one lateral hole, through which was passed a handle with sucking tube. — It was not, moreover, as he asserts (p. 395_{14}) "made to order especially for his [Petersen's] collection, on the model of a type then obsolete", for Hr. Petersen

---

[1] See my book (1914) pp. **339—340**, cf. **335—336**.

[2] Graah (1832) p. 140 cf my book (1914) p. 339.

[3] Rink, Grønland vol. II (1857) p. 359.

[4] The same applies to the Johan Petersen collection which at the end of 1910 came into the possession of our Ethnographical Department — „and since then I have not had the opportunity of seeing it" (My book, 1914, p. **325**).

could not possibly have "ordered" a type of implement which he had never known or heard of[1].

I have indicated this wooden bottle from Ammassalik as being "not typical, rather quite unique." Hr. THOMSEN does not venture on his own account to deny this, but contents himself with quoting a statement by JOHAN PETERSEN which he is thus not obliged to answer for, and possibly does not agree with. But even if the imitated wooden bottle found at Ammassalik by JOHAN PETERSEN should support Hr. THOMSEN's theory of the wooden bottle as an old-fashioned article (the eldest known specimen is that acquired by the Museum from 1848, whereas that in the Johan Petersen collection is a new product of different shape, and these are the only two known), it might well be correct that the other objects, which I have in this connection indicated as "not typical, rather quite unique", are so. I had here in mind the three objects which are described immediately after the wooden bottle in my book; a sucking tube for drinking water, and two wooden pails for drinking water, both belonging to HOLM's collection (Figs. 274 and 275 a and b). One of these wooden pails is made from a piece of a bamboo pole, and is absolutely unique. But also the two others are without parallel in our finds and collections, and I must still maintain that they are at any rate "not typical"[2].

I might here pass on from these pages of Hr. THOMSEN's paper, were it not that he has, on p. *394*, at the bottom, smuggled in a remark which, taken together with the footnote, is intended to have the effect of an insinuation. Without actually saying what he means, he slips in a comment altogether irrelevant to the question, on the fact of my having rendered some assistance to Kolonibestyrer JOHAN PETERSEN when he was seeking, after his return from Ammassalik in 1909, to dispose of his collection to a foreign Museum. Hr. THOMSEN writes as follows: "The expression 'Mikeeki's waterscoop etc.' is incomprehensible to the uninitiated, referring as it does to the unpublished catalogue of a pri-

---

[1] In order to avoid misunderstanding, I think it well here to call attention to the fact that Hr. Thomsen's fig. 1 (p. *395*) does not represent the dipper in question (No. 213), but is of quite a different and far more common shape. I did not make use of this last from the Petersen collection for my book, having already illustrated a similar form from previous collections (fig. 263 a in my book).

[2] Hr. THOMSEN appears to have misunderstood my words in the text: "These objects (the wooden bottle etc.) show us" — as if they applied to the JOHAN PETERSEN collection, whereas they referred to the objects I had illustrated in my book, viz. figs. 273, 274 and 275, which are described before and after the mentioned words. I may admit that the sentence is unfortunately placed, and might better have stood after the description of the whole. On the other hand it seems to me that both my parenthesis (the wooden bottle) and the expression "show us" distinctly indicate which objects I referred to.

vate collection which the Editor was at that time endeavouring to dispose of abroad"[2]". — Hr. THOMSEN's inverted commas after "abroad" are due to a slip or error of his own, for it is not, of course, his intention to give any citation or to accuse any other of having disposed of the collection, but me. As to his note 2, see p. *394*.

My assistance in the matter consisted solely in recommending this collection, and was but a natural expression of gratitude on my part for the untiring assistance which Hr. JOHAN PETERSEN had rendered me during my winter at Ammassalik, and for his courtesy in permitting me to photograph his collection for publication. With the practical side of the business, however, I had nothing whatever to do. I need not add that Hr. JOHAN PETERSEN had made his collection at his own expense and that he, as a matter of course, had his hands free in disposing of it.

The manner in which JOHAN PETERSEN's collection was finally disposed of (in December 1910) is an open secret. The Director succeeded, in a way which can not exactly be characterized as considerate, in bringing pressure to bear upon Hr. JOHAN PETERSEN (then a subordinate official in the service of the State) whereby it became possible for the Director to procure this valuable collection for his Museum. As a result of this inconsiderate and offensive treatment, the owner of the collection obtained exactly half the sum which he had asked (and could easily have obtained) abroad. — To avoid any misunderstanding on the part of readers unacquainted with the exact conditions, I may here call to mind that JOHAN PETERSEN's position as an official in Greenland did not involve any sort of obligation towards the Museum; on the contrary, the Museum had for years been indebted to him for repeated consignments, comprising not only specimens which he had been commissioned to procure, but also others voluntarily contributed by him[1]. And I may also point out, that many foreign museums actually possess ethnographical collections from Greenland, and even from Ammassalik itself, which have been procured at some time or other through Danish officials in this our Arctic colony[2]. Hr. JOHAN PETERSEN was naturally as free as his colleagues in regard to disposing of his collection. It would certainly seem that the Director of our Museum Department must have been aware of these facts when he entered upon a transaction of this nature.

In this manner then, the Director succeeded in obtaining for his Museum a valuable collection at a low price. Hr. THOMSEN is perfectly correct in stating that I was not unacquainted with the (scientific) value of the collection; his next remark, however, is somewhat surprising. If the Museum ethnographers took it for granted that JOHAN

---

[1] cf. THOMSEN p. *382*[10-13].

[2] See my book (1914) p. **326** and **669—70**.

Petersen did *not* know "its importance to the Danish Museum" (footnote p. *394*) we can better appreciate the clever manner in which this circumstance was turned to account by the Director in his endeavours to procure the collection and give as little as possible for it.

This is the first Greenland collection of any importance which the Museum has actually purchased. Up to that time, the Ethnographical Department had shown but slight interest in its rich Greenland collections, or indeed in the ethnography of Greenland at all. There is absolutely no reason for the authorities to be surprised at the fact that the collector finally preferred to offer the last of his collections to another Museum, more especially since it consisted mainly of duplicates of specimens which he had previously sent to the Danish Museum.

It is indeed remarkable altogether that the Ethnographical Department of the Museum should venture to touch upon the question of moral obligations in the case of its relations with a man who, independently of the Museum, interested himself in ethnographical work, and who had made considerable sacrifices in order to save the last remains of native culture for the cause of science. In the ethnographical sphere, the Department has to a regrettable degree lacked initiative. To quote but a single example; it was not at the initiative, or with the support, of the Department, that its cases came to contain what is now the classical base of all collections from East Greenland. Why has there not long since been set on foot a collecting enterprise in West Greenland similar to that of G. Holm at Ammassalik? How much is now irretrievably lost to science in this sphere, owing to the lack of understanding or of will in the central organ?

I felt this strongly myself when, in 1900, I visited the ruins and refuse-heaps of *Sermermiut* at the mouth of the great icefjord near Jakobshavn; when I later passed the site of the well known *Qeqertaq* finds in the innermost corner of Disco Bay; and when I wintered in the deep fjords of the *Umanak* and *Egedesminde* districts, where great quantities of ruins, graves and kitchen-middens testify to the ancient Eskimo occupation. These are the regions where our countryman, Dr. Pfaff, a generation ago got together his great and unique collection of Eskimo antiquities, which, after having been rejected by the Danish Museum, were sold to a Swedish patron of science, and are now in the possession of the Ethnographical Department of the Riksmuseum at Stockholm[1]. There are always a number of private persons or state employees eager to procure curiosities of this sort, but it would surely seem that our National Museum, as an ethnographical centre, should long since have been foremost among those interested in such collection work, and for ethnographical research work in Greenland generally.

In our day, when so many regions of primitive culture are being destroyed or undergoing change, ethnographical museums have every-

[1] See Medd. om Grønland, 39 (1914) p. 669.

where considered it their duty to collect material, and this applies not least to museums in smaller countries which have the good fortune through their government to stand in relation with the colonies of their own land. As far back as 1887 the Danish ethnographer K. Bahnson trenchantly observed that "the museum which fails to avail itself of the present time bars the way to its own development"[1]. And from this point of view, he notes the rich material from Greenland in the Copenhagen Museum, especially Holm's collection from East Greenland, but criticises sharply, on the other hand, the inadequacy of the exhibits intended to represent West Greenland culture in the Museum. "From the West Coast, we still lack a collection made with the same degree of thoroughness as Holm's. True, there is a considerable amount of material from this region in the Museum, but a number of the details which make our view of the East Greenlanders' life so vivid are absent in the case of the West Coast, although this part of the country has been far longer known to us. Now that Holm has led the way, it can scarcely be long before a similar systematic collection is made on the West Coast, especially in the northern districts, where the inhabitants are nearer now to their former state in this respect than is the case farther south. It is a national duty to have Greenland represented in exhaustive completeness, since Denmark is the only country having the opportunity of collecting there, and Greenland, moreover, is our most remarkable colony".[2]

At the Meeting of the Landsraad in South Greenland on the 2 September 1913, the Inspector of South Greenland as Chairman and some of the native representatives, on the occasion of the debate which had arisen concerning the preservation of culture memorials from Greenland, put forward a sharp criticism of the passiveness which the Danish National Museum up to that time had exhibited with regard to the work in Greenland, and laid down at the same time the plan for the Greenland Museum at Godthaab, which it has now been decided to erect[3]. And finally, in 1916, a circular was issued by the Danish State,

---

[1] K. Bahnson, Etnographiske Musæer i Udlandet (in Aarböger for nordisk Oldkyndighed, 1887, p. 179).

[2] Cf. ibid. pp. 196—197.

[3] Beretninger og Kundgørelser vedrørende Styrelsen af Grønland No. 2, 1914 p. 194—195. — The Chairman of the South Greenland Landsraad stated under discussion of point 11 of the proceedings as follows: He wished to draw attention to the fact that the question only of late years had become one of present moment, as it had been found that both foreign visitors and Danish residents in Greenland systematically and without any consideration caused old graves to be plundered and their contents scattered abroad. He was keenly interested in the plan for preserving the old memorials of former culture, but he considered it unreasonable that grave finds should be handed over to the National Museum, and was surprised at the sudden interest now exhibited by the Museum, which had never before attached any importance to the question. Instead of entering into communication with the Danish residents, the Museum had remained passive, and had thus permitted the greater

with reference to Greenland, in which certain restrictions are imposed upon officials and others in the Danish parts of the country with a view to preserving the ancient cultural remains. The debate in the South Greenland Landsraad in 1913 did not pass unnoticed in Denmark, where the scientific research in Greenland, both as regards the country and the natives, has never lacked friends. Under pressure of circumstances then, the ethnographers of the National Museum found themselves at last obliged to recognise the fact that they also had certain duties to consider in our distant possession. Unfortunately, it seems beyond all doubt that the Museum has been somewhat tardy in coming to this conclusion, so that certain of the more perishable objects in Eskimo culture which were still obtainable a generation or less ago, are now no longer to be procured. There are others, private visitors, officials in the country, or even functionaries in subordinate administrative positions, who have attempted to carry out some part of the honest task in Greenland, but without any assistance from the expert knowledge of the Museum. And a great deal of scientifically valuable material has thus passed out of the country (Greenland).

It must thus appear the more unjustifiable for the Museum now to take up the cause of moral obligation against a private collector who, as in the present case, had for years rendered the Museum valuable service. In the name of science it should long since have been demanded that the First Department of our National Museum itself, by one or more expeditions to Greenland, set about the great systematic research of the ethnography of this distant colony which up to the present has never been made.

Whetting Irons.

p. *396—98*. Here, as again and again throughout the work, Hr. THOMSEN's criticism is raised against an instance where I have expressed a certain critical doubt, or advanced another explanation than my predecessor, or ventured upon some hypothesis, or indicated the possible solutions which occur to me, where a single categorical assertion would appear to be misplaced. There is nothing in my doing so which

---

part of the objects hitherto brought to light to be acquired by foreign countries.

He therefore considered it more proper to establish a Greenland Museum which should have the first claim to anything which might be found in graves or of remains from the time of the Norsemen.

Several of the native members then rose to support the motion. One of these, the Member for the 1st Division (JOSVA KLEIST, Frederiksdal) spoke as follows: He agreed with the idea, and likewise considered it unreasonable that the grave finds from Greenland should be allowed to go out of the country. The Greenlanders had no other history than that which the graves could show, and it was important that the people should be able to see the weapons and implements formerly in use, that they might learn in what manner their forefathers had lived.

offends against the general scientific practice, indeed the contrary is the case. I have at times been rather too conscientious than the reverse, with regard to expression of doubt or indication of possible solutions. Is it possible that Hr. THOMSEN can be quite a stranger to this method of treating scientific questions?

A remarkable object like the whetting iron resembling a drill in HOLM's collection led me to seek for something similar within the Eskimo regions. I believe that any unprejudiced reader, on going through the literature of Eskimo ethnography with me, would be willing to admit that no implement illustrated there shows a greater degree of similarity to HOLM's whetting iron than the drill shaft from Baffin Land to which I have referred, and which Hr. THOMSEN has considered worth while reproducing in his illustration. The similarity is present with regard to the features pointed out, and we have then the difference, that the shaft in the one case has a row of narrow grooves, in the other a single broader one. That the end of the Greenland implement is blunt, and not sharp like that of the drill, could of course easily be explained as due to fragmentary state of the object, more especially since the corresponding duplicate in HOLM's collection has a more or less pointed end.

My critic has evidently felt hurt at my having ventured to suggest that the explanation given by HOLM of these two pieces in his list, and in agreement with JOHAN PETERSEN, might possibly be incorrect, and that the original purpose of the implement could perhaps be viewed in another light if compared with related forms from other regions, as for instance the drill from Baffin Land. This was only intended as a modest suggestion, which might eventually lead to an explanation of the question as to how these unique Greenland implements had come to their remarkable appearance. Naturally, I never intended to put forward any emphatic denial of the correctness of the explanation already handed down, nor was it my purpose to give any final explanation as to the original use to which the implements had been put[1].

With regard to the "whetting stone" in my book, which Hr. THOMSEN, despite my doubts, maintains to be of iron and not of stone, whereas I myself, after seeing and handling the object in the Museum, came to the conclusion that it was of stone, I see no reason to carry discussion further in these pages. But the matter might well be deserving of further investigation.

p. *398—99.* — Hr. THOMSEN at times, in his eagerness to pick out quotations from my book, uses my words as his own. In this case he

[1] Hr. THOMSEN has himself elsewhere taken a similar liberty; on p. *429* (ad Fig. 231 a) he expresses a doubt as to a statement made by G. HOLM. The implement noted by HOLM as a "skin creaser" Hr. THOMSEN here prefers to regard as a "toggle" (his words are: "it was, however, doubtless intended as a toggle on some line").

is simply repeating a correction which I myself had made, the correction on my part being naturally due to my co-operation with the natives, or notes from the time of my stay, and not museum studies.

A mere reiteration of this nature would surely seem to be superfluous.

An Eskimo work of Art.

p. *399—400.* — With regard to Hr. THOMSEN's note as to this, I would first of all observe, that his characterisation of the two faces must be taken on his own responsibility; and further, that he entirely ignores my principal statement. I emphatically pointed out that we have here "the only really old evidence of the occurrence of masks or mask-like objects in Greenland". The remainder is based upon mere conjecture as to the purpose of the objects, and I have left the question open. It should in this connection be noted, that the object is only a fragment, the neck of the head being broken, and there is nothing to preclude the supposition that it may have been placed on a memorial post several feet high such as those described by NELSON from South-West Alaska[1].

I admit that my memory here played me false, so that I referred to the object as a grave find, whereas the inventory lists record it as found on the excavation of an old house, evidently owing to the fact that the carving of the wooden block was done during winter in the house in question. This need not, however, contradict my explanation of the purpose for which it was intended.

Wooden Dolls.

p. *400—402.* — My reference to RYDER and GRAAH is in connection with a sentence in my book reading as follows:

"As already mentioned the wooden dolls of the Ammassalik children must be considered in the main as toys but it is possible, that by the grown-up people they were formerly given a significance beyond their capacity as playthings"[2].

---

[1] NELSON writes: (l. c. p. 318—319) that it was the custom south of the mouth of the Yukon river "to erect memorial posts for all people who die in such a manner that their bodies are not recovered (e. g. drowned at sea, or buried by a landslide in the mountains"). At the annual feast for the dead, sacrifice is made to the figure of the deceased, and a new coat placed on the figure. In addition to the fact that "a number of small wooden figures" might be erected at the grave "in honor of people whose bodies were lost" we have the occurrence, for instance, at a grave at *Tununek*, of a single "post" upon which were "nine images of the large hair seal" in a row, i. e. miniature bodies no larger than the double mask found in East Greenland.

[2] "RYDER (1875) pp. 139—140; GRAAH (1832) p. 101". Quotation from Meddelelser om Grønland 39, pp. 644—645.

It will be seen that we have here a problem as to the solution of which there may be some doubt; now, the dolls are playthings and nothing else, but there may be some reason to suppose that they were formerly regarded in a different light, at any rate by adults.

Hr. THOMSEN cannot deny that both GRAAH and RYDER here found a similar problem, and that this is plainly evident from the passages in their books to which I refer and which he partly quotes. These writers have taken up the same question as I myself; GRAAH very briefly, RYDER more in detail, and Ryder ends by asserting that the dolls are now at any rate only playthings for children.

Hr. THOMSEN, however, is evidently anxious to find me guilty of misquotation or some other misdemeanour; at any rate he makes desperate efforts to obscure one side of the opinion expressed by the writers in question and emphasise another, by quoting the respective passages and setting certain sentences in spaced type as if in the hope that these may at a hasty reading produce a different impression in the reader's mind. And finally he omits the one sentence in RYDER's observations which would most of all serve to damage his case. RYDER states clearly as follows: "The wooden dolls are *now* used by the natives of Angmagsalik only as toys for children"[1]. And a little farther on we read, at the conclusion of the whole discussion:

"Selvom der derfor muligvis engang i Fortiden har været en eller anden højere Tanke forbundet med disse Dukker, hvad jeg for min Del efter det foran anførte meget betvivler, saa er Dukkerne for de nuværende Beboere af Angmagsalik kun Børnelegetøj".

[Translation:] "Even if there may possibly, at some time past, have been some higher idea connected with these dolls, which I for my part, after what has already been stated, am much inclined to doubt, for the present inhabitants of Angmagsalik the dolls are only playthings". — RYDER.[2]

The problem does not appear altogether the same to GRAAH as to RYDER; the former writer has found some "dolls" in an East Greenland grave, and asked himself whether they are "idols" like those which the savages presented to the Danish discoverer of Bering Straits; the latter finds the dolls in possession of children, and is reminded of the well-known amulet dolls which we have found at Ammassalik. Despite this, both reject the idea that the dolls found should be other than playthings; RYDER, however, with a certain hesitation, considering it not impossible that such may have been the case in former times. I am thus certainly justified in referring to these writers as to men who have considered the question, quite apart from the fact that I have in my own

[1] This sentence from RYDER's paper is found in Hr. THOMSEN's quotation, see p. *401*. The italics in *now* are mine.

[2] RYDER, Beretning om den Østgrønlandske Expedition 1891—92 (Medd. om Grønl. 17), p. 141. — This passage Hr. THOMSEN omits in his quotation p. *401*.

investigations later on come to a conclusion which suggests the probability of this alternative, that "there may possibly at some time past have been some higher idea connected with these dolls".

That the dolls used by children as playthings are different from those used by the Ammassalimmiut as amulets or idols I have myself also pointed out in my book (pp. **644—646**), but I leave open the possibility that the dolls may in the parents' eyes have been connected with some religious principle or custom. Many other sides of the Eskimo life and property have been subjected to the control of religion or magic[1].

Hr. THOMSEN may therefore enjoy his irony by himself, and pocket his insinuation again. Once more his hypercritical zeal has overshot the mark.

p. *402*[13], read "seemingly" instead of "evidently".

Jointed Dolls.

p. *402—404*. — Parturiunt montes. Hr. THOMSEN appears greatly upset by the fact of my having compared the finds of dolls with movable joints at Ammassalik with similar finds made among the Eskimo's neighbours in Asia, and combining this fact with the theory of marked conservatism in this race, which has given rise to so many other similarities in the culture of the western and eastern Hyperboreans.

I am certainly justified in offering a warning against drawing hasty conclusions as to "European influence"in cases such as this. It is Hr. THOMSEN and not I who drags in the jointed dolls of ancient Greece.

I have, by the way, on other occasions pointed out, that we might expect to find — and as a matter of fact actually do find — traces of European influence reaching even as far as Ammassalik by way of the south, and this already in times long past (e. g. my book p. **719**, cf. p. **332—339**, **471**, **486—487**, **668** and **682**). In this instance, however, I have not deemed it necessary to have recourse to such explanation.

I have had two examples of dolls with movable joints on which to support my view, both from Ammassalik, one belonging to the Greenland Administration collection (see fig. 368 b in my book 1914, p. **647**) and one in the National Museum, belonging to the Thalbitzer collection there (not illustrated). Hr. THOMSEN further mentions seven specimens, likewise from Ammassalik, all "jointed at the knees", which I did not succeed in discovering at the Museum. I myself have had since the good fortune to make the acquaintance of yet another wooden doll, with movable hip-joints, belonging to JOHAN PETERSEN's latest private collection (Fig. 1 in this paper). We have thus altogether ten wooden dolls with movable joints from Ammassalik. The last specimen was found by some native hunter belonging to the family of MARATTE, near

[1] The same is true of their tattooing, vid. the remarks of HOLM in "Den danske Konebaads-Expedition" pp. 227—228.

Kialineq, far to the north of Ammassalik, where the family in question wintered during the year 1912—13 after the district there had not been visited by any of the natives since 1882. The wooden doll here found thus dates from the time prior to the arrival of Europeans at Ammassalik, and supports the impression that dolls of this sort were made by the Greenlanders in ancient times.

If Hr. THOMSEN could find some means of proving that the wooden objects in my fig. 241 are implements of an old Eskimo type, and ex-

Fig. 1. Wooden doll with movable hip-joints, from Kialineq, East Greenland. Johan Petersen priv. collection. 1/2.

plain their use, he would be doing something more useful than when counting the holes in them. We find, by the way, mention of a wooden almanac with nine holes in the old Journal of P. EGEDE[1].

Shark's Tooth Knives.

p. *404*. — It is quite correct that Olearius writes *Ekulugsua*, but the word as thus given in his original work itself contains a printer's error; his *Eku-* must doubtless be meant for *Eka-* (he spells, in German fashion, all substantives with an initial capital); in the language of

[1] P. EGEDE, Journal, (1788) p. 79: "for I had made as many holes as there were days until the 9th January" (i. e. nine) "on a small piece of board, with a peg to move each day".

today the word is spelt *ekalugssuak*. In my quotation from OLEARIUS an additional printer's error has unfortunately crept in.

p. *405*. — Hr. THOMSEN's remarks anent my observations on the shark's tooth knives seem to me to be somewhat superfluous, and in part irrelevant. He points out, quite correctly, that shark's tooth knives can be single-edged[1]. But my description of the double-edged shark's tooth knives, which are of far more frequent occurrence than the former type, is in accordance with the facts, and the knives with stone cutting edges from Southampton Island I have myself referred to. (Our European distinction, by the way, between the two materials, metal and stone, would hardly be understood by the Eskimo, who have never been in contact with European culture; to them iron is probably merely a kind of stone). — The paper by JAPETUS STEENSTRUP, to which Hr. THOMSEN refers in this connection, I have myself also quoted, viz; on p. **488** in my book, where I dwell on the knives described by STEENSTRUP from West Greenland, made with small "iron plates which were fixed in a groove along the edge of a bone haft"; i. e. resembling the Australian native type of knife (or saw) with a row of small flint flakes set in a resinous mass along a handle[2].

Hr. THOMSEN concludes with some fantastic conjectures as to what he imagines to have been my object in mentioning the ethnographical parallel.

Umiak cleaner or boathook.

p. *406*. — An umiak or a kayak intended for paddling about among the ice-floes of the East Greenland sea might well find some use for a boathook, and even a short one would be handy at times. The so-called umiak cleaners (HOLM) are known only from Ammassalik, whereas boathooks of similar form, but longer, are well known among the Labrador Eskimo, and now also from West Greenland (see PORSILD 1915, p. 247).

Harpoons.

p. *407—408*. — In my book (1914, p. **411**) I raised the question of a detail in the technical construction of the harpoon, to wit, the method of joining the foreshaft and the loose shaft, as my experience in East Greenland did not bear out the earlier description of this point given by OTIS MASON. I therefore directed my criticism towards this writer, albeit with all due respect for his ethnographical work, and Hr. THOMSEN admits that I am right thus far. On the other hand, I may acknowledge that I was beyond the mark in supposing that my criticism could also be extended to apply to the harpoons from the West Coast

[1] See Medd. om Grønland, vol. 10, Pl. XXVI.

[2] BAHNSON, Ethnografien, vol. I, 18 (fig. 11, c).

of Greenland; these are, on closer examination, found to answer to MASON's description[1].

It is a satisfaction to me to note, that my having touched upon this detail in the structure of the harpoon has already induced three ethnographers to take up the matter for discussion. One of them has already criticised another on the same point[2] and assisted him to a correction. As it is, I admit, that MASON's error has proved to apply only to the harpoons of the East Coast, not for those of the West Coast, his description of these latter being correct. To make quite sure, I satisfied myself on the point by personal observation when travelling on the southern part of the West Coast in the summer of 1914.

As regards the harpoons of the East Coast, my description is correct.

p. *409—410*. — My Museum critic is a past master in the art of employing quotations dissociated from their proper context. His paper contains many instances of this. In the natural light in which they appear in my book, these passages are free from the false reflections, and the criticism does not hit the mark.

Contents Lists of the Collections.

p. *410—416*. — The pedantic acerbity of the Museum official rises in the following pages to an astonishing degree.

The reader will naturally expect" etc. (p. *410*). I can only repeat what I have already stated on p. 448 (with note) and p. 456: that I never intended my work to give either more or less than it contains. With regard to the genesis of my book, the reader may refer to the preface (in 1914) and to pp. 442—46 of the present paper. From this, as from the work as a whole, it will be seen that I am not a representative of any museum, least of all our own National Museum, and it would thus be altogether outside my province to publish the lists of the Museum collections in my book, or subject myself to the principles of that institution. Hr. THOMSEN's objections to my arrangement of these matters appear to me as extraordinary as they are improper.

It is obviously the duty of the Museum, and no business of mine, to publish inventories of the collections in its care. The Museum has

[1] In taking up this matter for the first time, I kept in the main to my experience in East Greenland. During my previous stay in West Greenland, I had not devoted any attention to this slight detail. Nor had I in the museums examined the harpoon shafts especially as to this detail, which is hidden between the two parts of the shaft, as it is my habit to observe great care in the handling of museum exhibits. The highly dried specimens, both thongs and other parts, near the junction of the shaft are generally brittle, and if I had attempted to bend the loose shaft over for examination, I should have risked a break at the joint. A Museum official, on the other hand, can take greater liberties with his material.

[2] See THOMSEN, p. 409 note 1.

now acquired JOHAN PETERSEN's collection, and might well publish the inventory list. As long as I had access to Hr. JOHAN PETERSEN's private collection, I could of course make use of his inventory with discretion, but I had neither the obligation, nor any right, to make it public. In the Museum, I had access to the Holm collection and others, but not to the inventory lists. For these and other reasons then, I considered it out of place to fill several pages of my work with the catalogue already published (in Medd. om Grønl. vol. X pp. 351—358); I contented myself with giving in extenso HOLM's introduction to his list (see my work 1914 p. **753**).

On the other hand I have of course the right, and excellent reason, to publish the inventory of my own collection, either in part or in full. To suggest that this should have been done at the expense of the lists for the Holm and Petersen collections is simply nonsense.

With an outward show of science, Hr. THOMSEN here endeavours to create the impression that a Museum Expert is now coming along to help us out. I do not think, however, that these specimens of inventory criticism will excite admiration outside the select circle of the Ethnographical Department, and it would perhaps have been well for the reputation of the gentlemen concerned had the criticism in question never appeared.[1]

p. *412*. As to the observation that "another scientific opinion pronounced it a hare" I am somewhat in the dark as to what is here intended, but it is doubtless of slight import. I had my information, as it happens, from a native Greenlander, who has himself seen the polar bear rear up on its hindlegs to defend itself against attacking dogs. And my informant is certainly more competent to judge than either the Museum official or his zoological friend.

p. *413—414*. Surely criticism such as this cannot be squeezed within the bounds of common fairness. If only as an example, it seems worth while looking into the manner in which Hr. THOMSEN deals with some amendments made by myself in the later list, or my own corrections of unavoidable misunderstandings in my earlier investigations.

In the course of my ethnographical studies, I gradually attained to a more correct appreciation of certain objects in AMDRUP's finds from the depopulated part of the East Coast, and was thus in 1914 able to put forward a more likely explanation of two or three implements than in 1909. Now, after having had the opportunity of consulting my final

---

[1] For those who have not time to look up the extensive references of my critic I would merely call to mind that a period of several years elapsed between the publication of "List I" 1909 and "List II" 1914, the latter being thus a revised, improved and augmented list. In the latter, moreover, it is naturally only a printer's error which gives the numbers of Figs. 56[1] and 56[2] as 561 and 562; Hr. THOMSEN, it would seem, was unable to realise this.

results, Hr. THOMSEN makes it appear as if it were he himself who had made the discovery, while as a matter of fact he has contributed absolutely nothing in any way whatever to the attainment of the correct conclusion. And he then goes on to apply his own particular art of critical quotation with the object of extracting the desired result from the actual process. As far as I can see, all that he really succeeds in doing is demonstrating clearly how far his method is removed from true scientific research; he has thus nothing but scorn for the gradual growth of a true solution, which, from its very nature must often follow a sinuous course, feeling its way by arduous work of which no trace appears in the simplicity of the final result. It would seem, however, that there will always be a class of men for whom only authorised and irrevocable opinions exist; who have never themselves experienced the inner metamorphosis of development.

Take another instance. In my book 1909, p. **441—443**, after a detailed description of the "wooden hammerlike implement (blubber beater?)" in List I, I added a few lines suggesting that the implement resembled in shape the post at the bottom of the stern of an umiak, *at the same time however, rejecting the possibility* that the specimen in question had any connection with such use. My critic, nevertheless, again finds an opportunity of distorting my meaning by an unfair dislocation of part of the text (p. *414* at bottom of page).

p. *415—416.* In 1909, the Commission for Investigations in Greenland presented my collection from Ammassalik to the Ethnographical Department. It was not a large collection, as my instructions for the winter's stay made no mention of ethnographical studies or collecting work. Nevertheless, this collection does contain certain rare or new items, of which the Museum did not previously possess any specimens from Greenland, such as wooden masks, a mask sewn of sharkskin, a decoy-whistle, a sling, spindle-buzzes, etc.; in a word, objects which warrant the assigning of some relative importance to the whole as compared with the principal collections from Ammassalik, on which I have largely drawn for my material. It is therefore ridiculous to insinuate, as the Museum critic suggests (p. *416*), that I have given too much credit to my own collection.

His futile attempt at making me responsible for the contents of the collection is easily disposed of. It is not my fault if the lists of the Department do not now agree with the collection which the Museum at an earlier date received with thanks. The list published by me is independent of that given by the Department, and is naturally correct. Hr. THOMSEN's suggestion p. *416* (at bottom of page) is altogether worthless.

IV. "Concluding Remarks".

The foregoing will, I trust, have made clear, by a close examination of Hr. THOMSEN's objections, that his criticism is prejudiced and essentially misleading, even though he may be right in regard to certain points. And as to the latter, I can hardly imagine that anyone will be surprised at the occurrence of errors in a work of so great extent, and partly, too, of a pioneering character, the more so since the writer has in various instances lacked the support of loyal assistance on the part of the Museum, where great treasures of ethnographical material have been suffered to repose in the obscurity of the unknown. It will easily be seen that most of the failings in my work could have been avoided if I had been effectively supported by the Museum at the time.

To answer every one of the objections which my critic has scraped together would be as fruitless as it is unnecessary. A criticism based, as this is, upon trifles, and having continual recourse to far-fetched arguments, veiled insinuations, to ways that are dark and tricks that are vain, is hardly calculated to inspire confidence.

The fact of the matter is, that this critical effort as a whole suffers from an inherent structural weakness, being directed towards two distinct ends; the one, under cover of a pretended scientific paper to justify the ways of the Museum to man; the other, to furnish expert information upon ethnographical questions. The quality of the expert information is not improved by this alliance. Hr. THOMSEN does not appear as one scientifically interested in the problems at issue, and has not in any single instance dealt honestly and positively with the subject matter.

p. *417*. — It is nothing less than an enormous exaggeration on the part of my critic to assert that he has only touched upon "indisputable errors". Save for his "corrections" of my references to the Museum collections and some few other amendments, he has not succeeded in deciding any point whatever. He has, however, in numerous cases demanded the impossible, the unattainable, by insisting on "definite results" even where the problem was that of some find not hitherto explained, some indefinable peculiarity in an implement, or a doubtful fragment. In such cases, any explanation offered must almost of necessity be "disputable".

The fact of the matter is, that I was the first to furnish accurate descriptions of numerous objects belonging to the material culture of Greenland, which have not previously been described in detail; some of them, moreover, being hardly known at all from the literature published up to that date. Not a few questions remained unsolved; others were answered by a probable hypothesis. In certain instances I have, after years of study and research, involving hesitation and careful consideration, finally arrived at a more correct solution. In my earlier works, I have frequently expressed a provisional opinion with regard to a problem hitherto unsolved, or an ethnographical point not previously described, correcting this in later publications when further study had placed me in a position so to do.

And in three cases at least I have myself corrected erroneous statements in the inventories of the museums[1].

But this is by no means the first time that Hr. THOMSEN has put forward an accusation against me which recoils upon himself or the Museum. The same may be noted with regard to what Hr. THOMSEN is pleased to call my "peculiar methods" etc. (p. *417*). I may here refer to my refutation of his assertions and my exposition of his own peculiar methods of dealing with museum studies (pp. 445 ff, 450 and 470 f.) as also with citations of my books (e. g. pp. 465 and 471) including his regrettable slips or printer's errors (pp. 452—53). I have no need of going farther into Hr. THOMSEN's treatment of his sources; his manner of dealing with one of his sources at any rate, to wit, my books, does not testify to any scientific spirit.

p. *417—422*. I have no desire to continue further the unravelling of this serpentine tangle. The pages here cited exhibit the same qualities as the foregoing, overloaded as they are with a tissue of heterogeneous remarks, observations, assertions and objections, unimportant, incorrect and prejudiced, or bearing evident witness to complete misunderstanding; most of them of an extremely petty character, albeit

---

[1] I am here referring, in the first place to my having demonstrated that the Eskimo bone tubes designated by the Copenhagen Museum as a kind of children's plaything (*ajagaq*) were in reality old-fashioned needlecases of a type once extensively in use (see my Description of the Amdrup Collection from East Greenland 1909, p. 422 and cf. my article in Baessler-Archiv, vol. II, 1911, p. 41 note 4). In the second place, to my correction of the Pfaff inventory with regard to heads of adzes from North-west Greenland: "three pieces for fastening the axe, two of them with a hole in the middle for insertion of the haft" ("tre stykker til øxens fasthæftning, med et hul i midten for de to stykkers vedkommende til anbringelse af skaftet") the text in inv. Pfaff 27 Pl. I in Stockholm Riksmuseum, Ethnographical Department. This was quoted without amendment in my paper of 1909, p. 526 but corrected in my later work p. **482**, note 1, to whaling harpoon heads, this being the real purpose for which the objects (figs. 101—102) were intended. The same correction has later been made by MORTEN PORSILD (Medd. om Grønl. vol. 51, p. 144), doubtless independently of mine. And thirdly, I corrected the Pfaff inventory's "toggle harpoons intended for sealing or salmon-spearing etc" likewise quoted by me without comment in 1909 (l. c. p. 500, ad figs. 79—80) to the true definition: hinged toggles for drag lines; this last correction will be found in my later work p. **433—34**. The same correction has been made by MORTEN PORSILD l. c p. 189—90, independently of mine.

their intrinsic insignificance is intended to be obscured by the prolixity with which they are set forth.

It will here suffice to observe, regarding p. *418*[13], that Hr. THOMSEN's list of so-called corrections consists for the most part of something other than what is generally understood by this favourite term of his, as already indicated in the foregoing (p. 441). Here we find in profusion the supplementary information from the inventory lists of the Museum, which I ought to have received long since.

I do not, however, intend here to go into the question as to whether this or that particular point on which Hr. THOMSEN is pleased to touch has been "disturbed" or "undisturbed by such hindrances as he claims to have met with in the Museum" (the expression used by Hr. THOMSEN p. *418*). I prefer to refrain from further discussion, and leave Hr. THOMSEN to his monologue in his own particular wilderness.

V. The Museum Critic and his Allies.

p. *422* ff. — Hr. THOMSEN has here evidently found an ally in his superior officer — if indeed the case should not rather be stated as the reverse. On this page, and those immediately following, I perceive a reply from the Director of the Ethnographical Department. The hands are the hands of Esau, but the voice is distinctly Jacob's.

But the fact that the Director has thus succeeded in publishing his retort in a paper apparently written by his subordinate, does not render his observations any more correct. I still maintain my standpoint as heretofore, and would merely add, that I am surprised at the importance which the Museum attaches to my brief remarks of 1912[1].

p. *422—423*. — My statement to the effect that only a part of the Greenland collections "are said to have been set up in cases" i. e. exhibited, calls forth a whole page of disclaimer from the Museum official, with two notes and a full page illustration — which last I have not seen up to time of writing. The defence here is the more remarkable from the fact of its commencing, as far as I can make out, with a concession: the Museum authority admits "the exception of supplementary specimens and fragments from the finds made on the sites of Eskimo villages which are placed in the window cupboards" — in other words it is acknowledged that a part of the material lies in the closed and locked cupboards beneath the windows. The scientist visiting the Museum could not divine the existence of this material, unless informed of it

---

[1] This portion of my book was printed in 1912, but the entire work was not published until 1914. — The remarks are cited here p. 438.

by some official of the Department. Only in such case can it be fairly said that these cupboards "are likewise accessible for scientific inspection" (THOMSEN, p. *422*, note 2).

It is a notorious fact, that parts of the Greenland collections, including HOLM's from Ammassalik, have been stored away from time to time. With regard to HOLM's collection, this was certainly stored away during the period immediately prior to 1898. I do not know whether this removal is or is not connected with that rearrangement of the Greenland collections which Hr. THOMSEN refers to as having taken place "some ten years back" — if so, the rearrangement must have been a somewhat lengthy process. Considerable portions of the old Greenland collections were not on exhibition during some of the first years of this century, and the visiting scientist could only obtain a sight of individual items on special requisition. Hr. THOMSEN maintains (last part of note 2, p. *422*) that when I spoke of HOLM's collection as having "lain in the Museum since 1888" it was my intention to imply that it had been on exhibition since that time. This is simply not correct. Where have I said any such thing? The fact just pointed out shows that a statement to that effect would have been untrue, while on the other hand I am perfectly justified in asserting that the collection has lain or been lodged in the Museum since that date without being continually on view.

I would further add, that Hr. THOMSEN vouchsafes no information whatever in answer to my observations concerning certain stone objects missing from the Holm collection, and not mentioned in the list given (cf. Medd. om Grønl. vol. 39, p. **493** and note 1).

With regard to Hr. THOMSEN's footnote p. *423* I would merely point out that a "letter forwarded by the Museum authorities" is not synonymous with an answer, and it was to an answer I referred in my book at the place quoted. There are letters which can be said to contain an answer, and letters which cannot be said to contain any answer at all.

I have thus had good grounds for my assertion above referred to anent the Greenland collections in the Museum. As a matter of fact, however, it was not my intention to imply that any blame should attach to the Museum on this account; naturally I know well enough that museums are often unable, from want of space, to set all their contents on view.

The illustration of the case containing the Ammassalik collection may perhaps be so cleverly contrived as to show the manner in which the exhibits are set up, but it cannot give a correct or an entire idea of the reality. I venture to maintain that a good photograph shows the objects more distinctly than reality, since the picture in a photograph is projected on a plane, whereas the actual perspective renders more distant objects less distinct. In any case, the illustration should render it easy to appreciate how difficult it would be, especially during the darker season, to get a view of objects placed at the back of the case, which is several metres deep, and with glass doors in which the light is refracted; also, how inaccessible the objects farthest in would be. Only the smaller items were placed on shelves: the larger weapons and dresses had to be removed one by one in order to be photographed, occasioning a great deal of awkward and unpleasant work for such of the Museum staff as were deputed to assist.

p. *424*[10ff]. — "a scientifically adequate arrangement of the collections etc." The view here taken by the Museum is unfortunately erroneous. The arrangement was as a matter of fact anything but scientifically adequate when it came to removing the objects systematically for scientific investigation. The method observed was exactly counter to the principle on which my removal of the objects must reasonably be based, and the difficulty of directing operations was doubled by the fact that I was not permitted to touch the objects before they emerged from the case. The items were by no means so arranged that they could be photographed shelf by shelf as they lay, or in the order in which they were placed against the rear wall or on the floor of the case.

"He was of course at liberty to have the same shelves removed for inspection as often as he might desire". A public authorisation to this effect from the Director would have been of great value to me if I had received it at the right time, during the course of my studies in the Museum. Now, however, I have no use for it.

p. *425*. — I never proposed to employ any other photographer than the one recommended by the Director, as I understood from what was said that it would be convenient to act in accordance with his suggestion. The solemn declaration on p. *425*[14] as to my having been "perfectly at liberty to engage another had I pleased" may doubtless be taken for worth as much or as little as the previous suggestions tending in the same direction. By way of guidance here, I may quote the following from Director MÜLLER's letter to me of 26-2-1910.

[Translation:] "Thanking you for your letter of 24th inst. I am able to inform you that the work of photographing may be commenced when you wish. Details can be arranged hereafter. If you do the photographing yourself, or employ a photographer known to the Museum, nothing more need be said. Should you wish, however, to have a photographer not generally employed in the Museum, I must reserve the right to consider the question".

We see then, that when the Director reserves the right to consider a question, he afterwards distinctly recollects having given the party concerned full liberty to make his own arrangements. Evidently there must be some special directorial conception as to what constitutes "full liberty".

This question however, was altogether of minor importance to myself, and I have never expressed any dissatisfaction with the Director's choice of a photographer.

p. *424—425.* — The Director is evidently at great pains to show — as he repeatedly attempts to hint throughout these pages — that I enjoyed, as a matter of course, the most complete freedom in his Museum. And here we approach very near to the crucial point.

Trifles, trifles; all these questions as to collections more or less fully on view, their arrangement, the time at which my work was permitted to commence, the choice of a photographer, and so on; things unimportant now as they were then. Whether I was granted scant or abundant time for the work to be done, if the light was good, bad or indifferent; all these are points of subordinate interest, and in part dependent upon personal estimate.

As a matter of course, I submitted punctiliously to all restrictions and regulations which were then in force at this Museum, and to which Hr. THOMSEN frequently refers in his critique. They were neither few nor inconsiderable in comparison with what I have experienced elsewhere; far from it[1]! Even so, however, the regulations, however strict, could hardly render my task altogether impossible. My ethnographical writings show that I did as a matter of fact succeed in getting nearly all the original photographs I wanted of the Greenland collections. What they do not show, is the price I had to pay for the acquisition of them.

If I was forced to desist from my work before it was completed, the reason is entirely independent of these impersonal regulations.

But here we verge upon the heart of the question.

A scientific authority proceeding upon principles calculated to destroy the mutual confidence which should exist between workers in the same field is and must ever be condemnable. —

p. *426.* — *Jam res ad triarios venit.* Hr. THOMSEN here seeks refuge in a coalition with the three he mentions.

They must be proud of the alliance.

---

[1] In the ethnographical Department of the Copenhagen Museum I had access to the collections only during the winter halfyear, and only three days a week, between 12 and 4. From May throughout the summer nothing was allowed to be removed from the cases, general visiting days being then more numerous than in winter. The objects had to be removed by one of the Museum staff, and the items I wanted had to be requisitioned in writing or pointed out the day before. Only one shelf at a time might be removed, and each day everything had to be put back in exactly the same order before 4 o'clock. etc. etc.

VI. List of "Corrections".

p. *426—434.* — By far the greater number of Hr. THOMSEN's corrections deal with my references to the names of the collections to which the various ethnographical items belong. I had noted every specimen in the large East Greenland case at the Museum which appeared to me typical of the Ammassalik culture as belonging to the "Holm coll." save where I had definite information to the contrary (cf. p. 447 and 450) since it was from HOLM's expedition that we first learned to know the central home of the Ammassalik tribe. In some cases I noted "Holm (?) coll." or "Holm and [or] other collections" etc. the latter where I knew or supposed that the specimens belonged to different collections. — My publication has finally served to elicit fuller information from the Museum inventories, and readers interested in matter of so minute detail — there will hardly be many — may now consult Hr. THOMSEN's "corrections". The importance of these is, however, somewhat diminished by the fact that he has in many instances been unable to identify the objects in question.

A small portion of his corrections refer to my measurements of the specimens, some few others to the material of which the objects are made. We have here one assertion against another. It is but natural, however, that an official having every facility for unlimited study at the Museum would be able to attain a higher degree of accuracy in various points of detail than a visitor less privileged in this respect.

Some few of the corrections serve at best but to furnish supplementary information, without contradicting my description, e. g. p. *428* ad **481** and **489.**

Finally, Hr. THOMSEN has here undertaken to correct certain printers' errors, especially the following:

Page in my work (1914)	Error.	Amendment
389$_2$	"... bow ..."	"... board ..."
476 note 6	VII	VIII
738^{25}	8	18
738^{9}	1885?	1885
739^{25}	1789	1689

To the remainder I append the following remarks:

[1) p. *427* ff. in Hr. THOMSEN's "Notes and Corrections" ad p. 389 in my book (1914)].

1) p. *427* ad **389.** — "The bird in question is a polar bear". The correction is very typical of Hr. THOMSEN's critical style. The object to which I refer is a claw (the nail itself), but possibly a closer investigation might be desirable, as an observer who is neither Eskimo

nor zoologist may easily confuse both beak and claws of a large bird with the claws of a bearded seal or of a young bear.

2) p. *427* ad **390**. — My critic's assertion to the effect that "it is the same object in both cases" is not correct. The object which he notes as Washington Museum No. 160.337 (i. e. No. 160337) has nothing to do with NELSON's Pl. LXXIX fig. 4, but is true of that writer's Pl. LIV fig. 10.

3) p. *427* ad **455**. — Here I would first of all call attention to the remarkable admission made by the Museum official: "The remainder" — of the content of my illustration — "is difficult to identify". This indistinguishabie remainder is a large double bladder with accessories, belonging to one of the collections in his Department of the Museum. The same difficulty is frequently apparent in the succeeding pages, and would seem to suggest a certain disorder somewhere in that Department.

Such a background is eminently calculated to emphasise the self-sufficiency with which the Museum official presumes elsewhere to judge my illustrations of objects selected by me for photographing in the Museum. In one case, (p. *428* ad **496**, see below, under 5) he even ventures to insinuate that the specimen in question is not from the Museum at all, despite my statement that it belongs to one of the collections there; this for the simple reason that he himself is unable to identify it. The same inability to recognise Museum property is exhibited in Hr. THOMSEN's comments p. *428* ad **497**, p. *431* ad **584** and p. *432* ad **611** etc.

His confession that he is in all these cases unable to identify Museum specimens certainly lessens our confidence in such identifications as he ventures to pronounce elsewhere. His observation p. *432* ad **645** likewise reveals a high degree of self-confidence, since he is here referring to something which he has not seen; cf. my note infra under (10).

4) p. *428* ad **476**. — The stone blades in the knives from Southampton Island are mentioned in my book p. **489** (below), cf. supra p. **468**.

p. *428* ad **478** 1) vide supra p. 463—64.
— - — 2) — — p. 462—63.
480 vide supra p. 462—63

5) p. *428* ad **496**. — "If preserved in the National Museum" etc. Here we have evidently an attempt at suggesting to the reader that I might have smuggled in extraneous material under the name of the Museum. As a matter of fact, I found these stones on one of the shelves in the Museum; where, may be seen from my book p. **493** (lines 4—7 from above). Cf. also HOLM p. **40** (mid).

6) p. *428* ad **497**. — I can find neither any correction nor anything new in these observations of the Museum official.

ad **502** whet stone or whetting iron? vide supra p. 463.

7) p. *429* ad **512** skin creaser or toggle? vide supra p. 463, note 1.
— ad **517** vide supra p. 467, with note.

8) p. *430* ad **552**. — The "correction" is probably incorrect. A small vessel like this, of the pertaq type, might very well be a drinking cup, cf. my book p. **557**, where my knowledge is more particularly based on material from American writers, among them MURDOCH p. 101. HOLM calls the vessel in question a *Bæger*, 'a beaker', 'goblet' (Medd. om Grønl. vol. X, Pl. XXX). It is possibly more luxuriously finished than is generally the case, but intended for scooping up water, or to drink from.

9) p. *432* ad **614**. — "and is part of the lock" etc. This is merely a repetition of what I have myself stated in the text (1914, p. **614**—**615**).

p. *432* ad **635** vide supra p. 455.
— - **636** — — p. 464.

10) p. *432* ad **645**. — NB. Hr. THOMSEN was on no occasion present during my photographing of the objects in the Museum. And the accuracy of his identifications from my illustrations is, as we have seen under (3), open to doubt.

p. *432* ad **647** vide supra p 466[13]
433 - **677** — — p. 468.
— - **678** — — p. 463—64.
— - **681** — — p. 466—67.
— - **682** — — p. 451—56.

11) p. *433* ad **725—28**. In these pages of my book I have recapitulated and emphasised what I have called the ethnographical provincialisms of the Ammassalimmiut, as they appeared at the time when the district was discovered, without regard to the genesis of single features. That this was my intention is clearly evident from my discussion of the subject on p. **729**, where I particularly presuppose a number of these features to be "old relicts" formerly more widely distributed in Greenland. Wherever I refer to them as "local inventions", I expess myself with more reserve, and even add: "A few more of the peculiarities mentioned as only known now from Ammassalik have certainly been used earlier on the other coast". This last point is illustrated by many examples. Among them I have also mentioned the working implements of the men and women (knives, ulos, etc.). The cross-shaped kaiakstand from the northern part of West Greenland I have mentioned not only on p. **387**, but also here p. **729**. I have noted this form as a provincialism at Ammassalik from the fact of its being still in general use there long after it had been relinquished in West Greenland.

In issuing my summary, I had also particularly aimed at eliciting information as to the corresponding features on the West Coast, and succeeded in so doing far sooner than I had anticipated. Almost immediately, as a matter of fact, the Head of the Danish Arctic Station at

Disko, Hr. MORTEN P. PORSILD, on receiving my work soon after its publication in 1914, directed his attention towards these parallels, and was at once able to publish his observations in a paper then going to print: "*Studies on the Material Culture of the Eskimo in West Greenland*" (Medd. om Grønl. vol. LI, separately printed 1915). His interesting information was inserted in some additional notes towards the end of the paper (q. v. pp. 239 ff., especially pp. 247—48) to which I am happy to refer. — I imagine that Hr. THOMSEN has found the material for some of his more fortunate comments in Hr. PORSILD's valuable work.

12) p. *434* ad **739**. My list of works is far from being exhaustive I mention, however, two under RYDER's name. The "*Beretning, etc*". added by Hr. THOMSEN I have also referred to twice in my text (1914 p. **382** note, and **645** note) and in the usual manner, stating name of author and date of publication.

I am happy to take this opportunity of referring also to the rich bibliography of Greenland ethnography etc. given by H. P. STEENSBY in his recent work on the Origin of Eskimo Culture (Medd. om Grønl. vol. 53, 1916, pp. 219—228) as also to the lists in C. M. FÜRST and F. C. C. HANSEN's monumental *Crania Groenlandica*, Copenhagen 1915.

p. *434* ad **743—53** vide supra p. 469—71.

— - **739**. As to SCHACHT, vide supra p. 454—56 and p. 478_8.

I am at a loss to understand what Hr. THOMSEN may have meant by suggesting (line 7) that "the rest may be dispensed with".

We have now learned, however, that a considerable portion of Hr. THOMSEN's work might well have been "dispensed with".

TRANSLATED BY W. J. ALEXANDER WORSTER
PUBLISHED AT THE EXPENSE OF THE CARLSBERG FUND

Lightning Source UK Ltd.
Milton Keynes UK
UKOW06f1428070216

267882UK00002B/28/P

9 788763 522700